46 Nordic-Style Patterns
for Girls, Boys, and Babies

# WINTER KNITTING

## *for Little Sweethearts*

Hanne Andreassen Hjelmås · Torunn Steinsland
*Creators of KlompeLompe*

Photography by Hanne Andreassen Hjelmås

SCHIFFER
CRAFT
4880 Lower Valley Road • Atglen, PA 19310

This edition copyright © 2024 by Schiffer Publishing, Ltd.

Translated from the Norwegian by Carol Huebescher Rhoades
Photography by Hanne Andreassen Hjelmås

Originally published as *Klompelompes Vinterbarn* © 2018, J. M. Stenersens Forlag AS, Oslo. © 2018, Hanne Andreassen Hjelmås and Torunn Steinsland.

Library of Congress Control Number: 2024932166

Designed by Anne Vines
Type set in Nimbus Sans

ISBN: 978-0-7643-6844-8
Printed in China

Published by Schiffer Craft
An imprint of Schiffer Publishing, Ltd.
4880 Lower Valley Road
Atglen, PA 19310
Phone: (610) 593-1777; Fax: (610) 593-2002
Email: Info@schifferbooks.com
Web: www.schifferbooks.com

For our complete selection of fine books on this and related subjects, please visit our website at www.schifferbooks.com. You may also write for a free catalog.

**Other Schiffer Craft Books by the Authors:**
*Knitting for Little Sweethearts,* ISBN 978-0-7643-5627-8

*All-Year-Round Knitting for Little Sweethearts*: 68 Patterns for Everyday, Parties, and Special Times, ISBN 978-0-7643-6507-2

*Summer Knitting for Little Sweethearts*: 40 Nordic-Style Warm Weather Patterns for Girls, Boys, and Babies, ISBN 978-0-7643-6606-2

**Other Schiffer Craft Books on Related Subjects:**
*Nordic Hands: 25 Fiber Craft Projects to Discover Scandinavian Culture,* Anita Osterhaug, ISBN 978-0-7643-6691-8

*Create Naturally*: Go Outside and Rediscover Nature with 15 Makers, Marcia Young, ISBN 978-0-7643-6434-1

*Weave It!: 15 Fun Weaving Projects for Kids,* Maria Sigma, ISBN 978-0-7643-6065-7

Schiffer Publishing's titles are available at special discounts for bulk purchases for sales promotions or premiums. Special editions, including personalized covers, corporate imprints, and excerpts, can be created in large quantities for special needs. For more information, contact the publisher.

We are always looking for people to write books on new and related subjects. If you have an idea for a book, please contact us at proposals@schifferbooks.com.

MIX
Paper | Supporting responsible forestry
FSC
www.fsc.org
FSC® C104723

# Contents

| | |
|---|---|
| Introduction | 5 |
| Abbreviations | 7 |
| | |
| Grandmother's Dream Cap | 9 |
| Grandmother's Dream Sweater-Jacket | 11 |
| Nordigjønå Cowl | 17 |
| Nordigjønå Cap | 18 |
| Easy Mittens | 20 |
| Nerigjønå Cowl | 22 |
| Nerigjønå Cap | 26 |
| Wing Dress | 29 |
| Wing Dress for Dolls | 34 |
| Dinosaur Onesie | 39 |
| Hubbabubba Cowl | 42 |
| Hubbabubba Cap | 44 |
| Super-Easy Poncho | 46 |
| Lighthouse Pullover | 51 |
| Blanket for the Smallest Ones | 54 |

| | |
|---|---|
| Dinosaur Pullover | 56 |
| Kurt Pants | 61 |
| Rambaskår Sweater-Jacket | 64 |
| Rambaskår Pants | 70 |
| Flutter-About Scarf | 74 |
| Olle Ball Cap | 76 |
| Wing Union Suit | 80 |
| Albertine Cap | 86 |
| Julie Turtleneck Pullover | 90 |
| Henry Felted Mittens | 92 |
| Dottie Deer Pullover | 94 |
| Little Troll Pants | 98 |
| Izzy Cap | 102 |
| Izzy Polar Bear Pullover | 104 |
| Kari Coat | 108 |
| Winter Sweet Skirt | 114 |
| Fluffy Bobble Pullover | 118 |
| Fluffy Bobble Pullover for Adults | 122 |

| | |
|---|---|
| Fluffy Bobble Doll's Jacket | 124 |
| Fluffy Bobble Sweater-Jacket | 126 |
| Fluffy Bobble Sweater-Jacket for Adults | 129 |
| Dinosaur Doll Onesie | 132 |
| Maiken Cap | 136 |
| Julie Tunic | 141 |
| Thick "Shoe" Socks | 145 |
| Big Sister's Cap | 148 |
| Dinosaur Union Suit | 152 |
| Dinosaur Earflap Cap | 156 |
| Cable and Rib Cap | 158 |
| Little Troll Doll Pants | 162 |
| Izzy Cap with Two Pom-Poms | 164 |
| | |
| Index | 167 |
| Acknowledgments | 168 |

# Introduction

Earlier this year, we published our book *Summer Knitting for Little Sweethearts*. The book had a different format to distinguish it from our first books, and it included only knit clothes for children. The theme was, as the title suggests, summer clothing. Now we've written a follow-up to it in a similar format, with a theme of winter clothes.

Where we live, winter can be anything from splashing rain and strong winds to freezing cold and a calm sea. We're familiar with winters with little snow and a lot of slush. And we enjoy them, whether they're days that are just cold enough to ensure that the snow stays on the ground, or cold enough for safe ice skating. No matter which, it's all a pleasure with warm, fine winter garments, mittens, cowls, and caps.

As most of you know, we love to knit caps and, in this winter book, you'll find plenty of new cap patterns, some easy and some a little more difficult. All the patterns list a level of difficulty. If you want something quick and easy, chose a level 1 design. If you prefer a more challenging knitting project, then find one at level 3.

We thought some of the designs were so pretty that we decided to write patterns for women and men as an extra bonus for those who miss designs for adults. And, as in the summer book, we've also included some patterns sized for dolls and bears.

We list the yarns that were used for the knits in the photographs, but because yarn companies change their lines, it's inevitable that some of the yarns may be discontinued. If you can't find the yarn noted, or if you have different preferences, simply use a similar weight and type of yarn.

There is often a lot of laughter when we have to come up with names for the patterns. It isn't always simple, and we can easily spend half an evening fooling around with suggestions. In this book, we decided to give the patterns names from our childhood memories of Kvalavåg, the town we grew up in. It has only one main road, which goes from one end of town to the other, in just two directions, down and northward. The caps and cowls in the book are named for this road. The only mountain in Kvalavåg, which seemed huge to us, but really is not perhaps what one would call a mountain, is Rambaskår. It has fine hiking trails and forests to climb in, and we named several baby garments after it.

It has been inspiring and fun to make new knitting patterns throughout this winter. We would love to see your color variations! We hope you'll comfort yourself with new KlompeLompe knitwear when next winter arrives.

## ABBREVIATIONS

### KNITTING

| | |
|---|---|
| as est | as established, that is, continue in pattern |
| BO | bind off (= British cast off) |
| CC | contrast color (pattern color) |
| ch | chain stitch (crochet) |
| cm | centimeter(s) |
| CO | cast on |
| dpn | double-pointed needle(s) |
| g | grams |
| k | knit |
| k2tog | knit 2 together = right-leaning decrease; 1 stitch decreased |
| m | meter(s) |
| M1 | Make 1 = lift strand between two stitches onto left needle and knit into back loop = 1 stitch increased; stitch is twisted |
| MC | main color (background color) |
| mm | millimeters |
| p | purl |
| pm | place marker |
| psso | pass slipped stitch over |
| rem | remain/remaining |
| rep | repeat(s) |
| rnd(s) | round(s) |
| RS | right side |
| sl | slip |
| sl m | slip marker |
| ssk | (sl 1 knitwise) 2 times, insert left needle into sts and knit together through back loops = left-leaning decrease; 1 stitch decreased |
| st(s) | stitch(es) |
| tbl | through back loop |
| WS | wrong side |
| wyb | with yarn held in back |
| wyf | with yarn held in front |
| yd(s) | yard(s) |
| yo | yarnover |
| * - * or ( ) | repeat the sequence between asterisks or parentheses |

### I-CORD

(see video at klompelompe.no)

With a dpn, cast on 3 or 4 sts. Knit the sts. *Do not turn. Slide the sts back to front of needle, bring yarn across WS, and knit the sts.*Rep from * to * until cord is desired length.

### KITCHENER STITCH

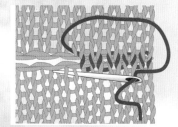

# Grandmother's Dream Cap

*Level 2*

**Sizes:** 0–1 (3, 6–9 months, 1–2, 3–6 years)

**MATERIALS**

**Yarn:** Sandnes Garn Børstet Alpakka (Brushed Alpaca) (CYCA #5 – bulky, 96% alpaca, 4% nylon, 120 yd (110 m) / 50 g)

Sandnes Garn KlompeLompe Tynn Merinoull (fine Merino wool) [CYCA #1 – fingering, 100% Merino wool, 191 yd (175 m) / 50 g]

**YARN COLORS AND AMOUNTS:**

Brushed Alpaca: Gray Heather 1042: 50 (50, 50, 50, 50) g

Tynn Merinoull: color A, Blue-Petroleum 7251 and color B, Putty 1013: 50 (50, 50, 50, 50) g of each color

**Needles:** U.S. sizes 2.5 and 8 (3 and 5 mm): 16 in (40 cm) circulars and sets of 5 dpn; optional: 32 in (80 cm) circular for magic loop

**Gauge:** 27 sts on smaller size needles or 16 sts on larger size needles = 4 in (10 cm).

Adjust needle size to obtain correct gauge if necessary.

The cap begins with the I-cord ties on the earflaps. An inner layer is worked first with the fine yarn, and then an outer layer is knitted with the brushed alpaca.

With Tynn Merinoull color A and smaller size dpn, CO 4 sts. Make an I-cord 7 in (18 cm) long.

**I-CORD**

With a dpn, knit the sts. *Do not turn. Slide the sts back to front of needle, bring yarn across WS, and knit the sts. *Rep from * to * until cord is desired length (see video at klompelompe.no).

The earflaps are worked in the round to make two layers. Now begin increasing for the first earflap:

*K1, M1*; rep * to * around = 8 sts (4 sts for back of flap and 4 sts for front). We recommend using the magic loop method (see video of technique at klompelompe.no) so you will have all the front sts on one needle and those for the back on the other needle. Or, you can place markers to separate the sides. Knit 1 rnd.
**Change to color B.
*K1, M1, knit until 1 st rem, M1, k1*; rep * to * on back. Knit 1 rnd.
Change to color A.
*K1, M1, knit until 1 st rem, M1, k1*; rep * to * on back. Knit 1 rnd.**

Rep these 4 rnds (** to **) until there are 48 (48, 52, 52, 56) sts or 24 (24, 26, 26, 28) sts for the front and 24 (24, 26, 26, 28) sts for the back. Set flap aside and make another cord and earflap the same way.

With smaller size needles and color next in stripe sequence: CO 3 (5, 7, 7, 10) sts, k24 (24, 26, 26, 28) sts of back earflap layer, CO 26 (32, 34, 34, 34) sts, k24 (24, 26, 26, 28) sts of back earflap layer and CO 3 (5, 7, 7, 10) sts = 80 (90, 100, 100, 110) sts total. Place front earflap layers on holders. Knit 1 rnd.

Work around in stripes (2 rnds color B – 2 rnds color A) until cap measures 3¾ (4¼, 4¾, 5¼, 6) in [9.5 (11, 12, 13, 15) cm].
On next rnd, begin shaping crown (change to dpn when sts no longer fit around circular);

**Decrease Rnd 1:** *K8, k2tog*; rep * to * around.
Knit 3 rnds in stripe sequence.

**Decrease Rnd 2:** *K7, k2tog*; rep * to * around.
Knit 3 rnds in stripe sequence.

**Decrease Rnd 3:** *K6, k2tog*; rep * to * around.
Knit 1 rnd in stripe sequence.

**Decrease Rnd 4:** *K5, k2tog*; rep * to * around.
Knit 1 rnd in stripe sequence.

**Decrease Rnd 5:** *K4, k2tog*; rep * to * around.
Knit 1 rnd in stripe sequence.

**Decrease Rnd 6:** *K3, k2tog*; rep * to * around.
Knit 1 rnd in stripe sequence.

**Decrease Rnd 7:** *K6, k2tog*; rep * to * around, ending with
k0 (4, 0, 0, 4).
Knit 1 rnd in stripe sequence.

**Decrease Rnd 8:** *K5, k2tog*; rep * to * around, ending with
k0 (4, 0, 0, 4).
Knit 1 rnd in stripe sequence.

**Decrease Rnd 9:** *K4, k2tog*; rep * to * around, ending with
k0 (4, 0, 0, 4).

**Decrease Rnd 10:** *K3, k2tog*; rep * to * around, ending
with k0 (4, 0, 0, 4).

**Decrease Rnd 11:** *K2, k2tog*; rep * to * around.

**Decrease Rnd 12:** *K1, k2tog*; rep * to * around.
Cut yarn and draw end through rem sts; tighten.

Weave in all ends neatly on WS.

Now pick up and knit sts around outside of cap with smaller
size circular. Beginning at center back, pick up and knit sts
in cast-on sts in same color as for beginning of lining and
knit held, front layer, earflap sts = 80 (90, 100, 100, 110) sts
total.

Continue in stripe sequence until you've worked 4 stripes.
Change to larger size needle and brushed alpaca.

Knit 1 rnd. Knit 1 more rnd, decreasing 30 (35, 40, 40, 44)
sts evenly spaced around = 50 (55, 60, 60, 66) sts rem.

Weave in Tynn Merinoull ends.

Knit around in stockinette for 3 (3¾, 4, 4¼, 5¼) in [7.5 (9.5,
10, 11, 13) cm].

**On sizes 6–9 months (1–2, 3–6 years):** decrease as follows:
*K4, k2tog*; rep * to * around.
Knit 2 rnds.

**ALL SIZES:**
**Decrease Rnd 1:** *K3, k2tog*; rep * to * around.
Knit 2 rnds.

**Decrease Rnd 2:** *K2, k2tog*; rep * to * around.
Knit 2 rnds.

**Decrease Rnd 3:** *K1, k2tog*; rep * to * around.
Knit 1 rnd.

**Decrease Rnd 4:** *K2tog*; rep * to * around.
Knit around on rem sts until you have made a tip about 3¼
in (8 cm) long.

Cut yarn and draw end through rem sts; tighten.

**FINISHING**
Weave in all ends neatly. Tack lining to outer layer with a few
sts. Knot the tip on top of cap.

Block cap by covering it with a damp towel; leave until completely dry.

# Grandmother's Dream Sweater-Jacket

After a request from a new grandmother for a cozy sweater with a striped hood, we designed this sweater-jacket. The sweater with clever details is oh so soft and light. On the matching cap, double-layer ear-flaps keep the cold away from sweet little ears.

*Level 2*

**Sizes:** 3 (6, 9 months, 1, 2, 4, 6, 8, 10 years)

**FINISHED MEASUREMENTS**

Chest: Approx. 20 (21¾, 22½, 23¾, 24½, 26½, 27½, 28½, 29¼) in [51 (55, 57.5, 60, 62.5, 67.5, 70, 72.5, 74) cm]

Total Length, *from shoulder down*: Approx. 9¾ (10¾, 11½, 13, 14½, 15½, 17¾, 19¾, 21¼) in [25 (27, 29, 33, 37, 39, 45, 50, 54) cm]

**MATERIALS**

**Yarn:** Sandnes Garn Børstet Alpakka (Brushed Alpaca) (CYCA #5 – bulky, 96% alpaca, 4% nylon, 120 yd (110 m) / 50 g)

Sandnes Garn KlompeLompe Tynn Merinoull (fine Merino wool) [CYCA #1 – fingering, 100% Merino wool, 191 yd (175 m) / 50 g]

**YARN COLORS AND AMOUNTS:**

Brushed Alpaca: Gray Heather 1042: 100 (150, 150, 200, 200, 200, 250, 250, 250) g

Tynn Merinoull

Colors A: Blue-Green 6571: 50 (50, 50, 50, 50, 50, 50, 50, 100) g

Color B: Blue-Petroleum 7251: 50 (50, 50, 50, 50, 50, 50, 50, 50) g

**Needles:** U.S. sizes 2.5 and 8 (3 and 5 mm): 24 in (60 cm) circulars and sets of 5 dpn; optional: 32 in (80 cm) circular for magic loop

**Notions:** 5 (5, 6, 6, 6, 7, 7, 8, 8) buttons

**Gauge:** 27 sts on smaller size needles or 16 sts on larger size needles = 4 in (10 cm).

Adjust needle size to obtain correct gauge if necessary.

The sweater begins with the sleeves, which are worked from the cuff up.

**SLEEVES**

With smaller size dpn and Tynn Merinoull color A, CO 32 (32, 36, 40, 40, 40, 42, 44, 46) sts. Divide sts onto dpn and join. Knit 13 (13, 13, 17, 17, 17, 17, 17, 17) rnds. Purl 1 rnd for foldline. Knit 14 (14, 14, 18, 18, 18, 18, 18, 18) rnds in stripes: 2 rnds color A, 2 rnds color B.

Change to larger size dpn and Brushed Alpaca. Knit 1 rnd. Knit 1 rnd decreasing 6 (6, 8, 10, 10, 10, 10, 10, 10) sts evenly spaced around = 26 (26, 28, 30, 30, 30, 32, 34, 36) sts rem.

82) sts evenly spaced across = 82 (88, 92, 96, 100, 108, 112, 116, 118) sts rem.

Continue in stockinette (knit on RS and purl on WS) until body measures 6¼ (7, 8, 9, 10¼, 11, 12¾, 13¾, 15) in [16 (18, 20, 23, 26, 28, 32, 35, 38) cm].

**Next Row (RS):** K17 (19, 20, 21, 22, 24, 25, 26, 26), BO 6 sts, k36 (38, 40, 42, 44 48, 50, 52, 54), BO 6 sts, k17 (19, 20, 21, 22, 24, 25, 26, 26).

On the next row, purl across, adding sleeves at underarms = 122 (132, 136, 144, 156, 164, 172, 180, 186) sts total.

Pm at each intersection of sleeve and body = 4 markers.

Now begin decreasing on every RS row:

**RS rows:** *Knit until 3 sts before marker, k2tog, k1, sl m, k1, sl 1, k1, psso*. Rep * to * across; knit to end of row = 8 sts decreased.

**WS rows:** Purl.

Rep these two rows until you've decreased a total of 9 (10, 10, 11, 12, 13, 14, 15, 15) times = 50 (52, 56, 56, 60, 60, 60, 60, 66) sts rem.

Purl 1 row on WS.

On next, RS, row, increase 10 sts evenly spaced across back (between the two center markers).

## HOOD
Work back and forth in stockinette until hood measures 9½ (9¾, 10¼, 10¾, 11, 11, 11½, 11¾, 12¾) in [24 (25, 26, 27, 28, 28, 29, 30, 32) cm] from last raglan decrease row.

**Next Row (WS):** Divide sts in half onto 2 needles. Turn hood wrong side out. With a third needle, join the two halves of hood with three-needle BO: K2tog, joining 1 st from each needle, *k2tog with 1 st from each needle; pass first worked st on right needle over 2nd. *Rep * to * until all sts are bound off.

## FRONT BANDS
With smaller size circular and Tynn Merinoull color A, beginning at lower corner of right front, pick up and knit 1 st in every st up right front edge, around hood, and down to lower corner of left front. Knit 1 row on WS.

Continue in stockinette until sleeve measures 5¼ (6¾, 7½, 8¼, 9¾, 11, 12¼, 13½, 14½) in [13 (17, 19, 21, 25, 28, 31, 34, 37) cm] from foldline.

*At the same time*, when sleeve measures ¾ in (2 cm) above foldline, begin shaping sleeve: K1, M1, knit until 1 st rem, M1, k1.

Increase the same way every 1¼ (1¼, 1½, 1½, 1½, 1¾, 2, 2, 2) in [3 (3, 4, 4, 4, 4.5, 5, 5, 5) cm] until there are 32 (34, 34, 36, 40, 40, 42, 44, 46) sts.

On last rnd, BO the first 3 and last 3 sts = 26 (28, 28, 30, 34, 34, 36, 38, 40) sts rem. Set sleeve aside and make second sleeve the same way.

## BODY
With smaller size circular and Tynn Merinoull color A, CO 138 (148, 156, 162, 168, 182, 189, 190, 200) sts. The first row = WS.

Knit 3 rows back and forth.

Change to larger size circular and Brushed Alpaca. Knit 1 row. Purl 1 row, decreasing 56 (60, 64, 66, 68, 74, 77, 80,

**Next Row (RS):** Knit, making 5 (5, 6, 6, 6, 7, 7, 8, 8) button-holes evenly spaced on left side. Buttonhole: BO 2 sts and, on next row, CO 2 sts over each gap. Place top buttonhole ⅜ in (1 cm) below first row of hood.

Knit 2 rows.

**Next Row (WS):** On front bands, BO knitwise to hood, knit across hood sts, BO rem front edge sts.

### LINING

With smaller size circular and Tynn Merinoull, over hood sts, beginning on RS, work back and forth in stockinette in stripe pattern (2 rows color A, 2 rows color B) for 7¼ (7¾, 8, 8, 8½, 8½, 8½, 8½, 9¼) in [18.5 (19.5, 20.5, 20.5, 21.5, 21.5, 21.5, 21.5, 23.5) cm].

**Next Row (WS):** Divide sts in half onto 2 needles. Fold hood lining with RS facing RS. With a third needle, join the two halves of hood with three-needle BO as above on hood.

### FINISHING

Sew tip of lining securely to tip of hood. Sew down lining along of lower edge, using brushed alpaca.

Using color A of Tynn Merinoull, sew a line of stitches through the lining and where you picked up sts to the ridges on the hood.

Fold in the single-color stockinette section of each sleeve and sew down on inside.
Weave in all ends neatly on WS. Sew on buttons.
Block sweater by covering it with a damp towel; leave until completely dry.

# Nordigjønå Cowl

In the countryside where we grew up, the road went in two directions. Hanne took this road when she visited Torunn, and we eventually called it Nordigjønå ("the north road"). An unusual name, perhaps, but with good memories for us. We named this cowl Nordigjønå, and it's easy as pie to knit.

---

*Level* 1

- - - - - - - - - - - - - - - - - - - - - - - - - - - - -

**Sizes:** 6–12 months (1–2, 3–6, 7–10 years, men's)

**MATERIALS**
**Yarn:** Sandnes Garn KlompeLompe Merinoull [CYCA #3 – DK, light worsted, 100% Merino wool, 114 yd (104 m) / 50 g]

**YARN COLORS AND AMOUNTS:**
Blue-Petroleum 7251: 50 (50, 50, 100, 100) g

**Needles:** U.S. size 4 (3.5 mm): 16 or 24 in (40 or 60 cm) circular

**Gauge:** 22 sts = 4 in (10 cm).

Adjust needle size to obtain correct gauge if necessary.

- - - - - - - - - - - - - - - - - - - - - - - - - - -

The cowl is worked in the round.

With circular, CO 84 (84, 96, 96, 108) sts. Join, being careful not to twist cast-on row; pm for beginning of rnd. Work following chart until cowl measures approx. 4¾ (6, 7, 8¾, 9¾) in [12 (15, 18, 22, 25 cm] in length.

Knit 1 rnd and then BO.

**FINISHING**
Weave in all ends neatly on WS.

Block cowl by covering it with a damp towel; leave until completely dry.

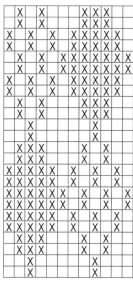

← begin here

☐ Knit on RS, purl on WS

☒ Purl on RS, knit on WS

17

# Nordigjønå Cap

*Level 1*

**Sizes:** 0–1 (3, 6–9 months, 1–2, 3–6, 7–10 years)

**MATERIALS**
**Yarn:** Sandnes Garn KlompeLompe Merinoull [CYCA #3 – DK, light worsted, 100% Merino wool, 114 yd (104 m) / 50 g]

**YARN COLORS AND AMOUNTS:**
Blue-Green 6571: 50 (50, 50, 50, 50, 100) g

**Needles:** U.S. sizes 2.5 and 4 (3 and 3.5 mm): 16 in (40 cm) circular; sets of 5 dpn; optional: 32 in (80 cm) circular for magic loop

**Notions:** Optional: faux fur pom-pom

**Gauge:** 22 sts on larger size needles = 4 in (10 cm).

Adjust needle size to obtain correct gauge if necessary.

With smaller size circular, CO 60 (68, 72, 84, 84, 88) sts. Join, being careful not to twist cast-on row; pm for beginning of rnd. Work 8 (8, 10, 10, 12, 12) rnds k1, p1 ribbing.

Change to larger size circular, Knit 1 rnd, increasing 0 (4, 0, 0, 12, 20) sts evenly spaced around = 60 (72, 72, 84, 96, 108) sts.

Work following chart.

**Note:** For sizes 0–1 and 3 months, work only part A.

After completing charted rows, continue in stockinette until cap measures 4 (4¼, 5¼, 5¾, 6¼, 7) in [10 (11, 13, 14.5, 16, 18) cm].

**Shape crown** (change to dpn when sts no longer fit around circular).

Knit 1 rnd, decreasing 0 (0, 0, 4, 0, 12) sts evenly spaced around.

**ALL SIZES EXCEPT 0–1 MONTH:**
**Decrease Rnd 1:** *K6, k2tog*; rep * to * around.

Knit 2 rnds.

**Decrease Rnd 2:** *K5, k2tog*; rep * to * around.

Knit 2 rnds.

**ALL SIZES:**
**Decrease Rnd 3:** *K4, k2tog*; rep * to * around.

Knit 2 rnds.

**Decrease Rnd 4:** *K3, k2tog*; rep * to * around.

**Decrease Rnd 5:** *K6, k2tog*; rep * to * around, ending with k0 (4, 4, 0, 0, 0).

**Decrease Rnd 6:** *K5, k2tog*; rep * to * around, ending with k0 (4, 4, 0, 0, 0).

**Decrease Rnd 7:** *K4, k2tog*; rep * to * around, ending with k0 (4, 4, 0, 0, 0).

**Decrease Rnd 8:** *K3, k2tog*; rep * to * around, ending with k0 (4, 4, 0, 0, 0).

**Decrease Rnd 9:** *K2, k2tog*; rep * to * around.

**Decrease Rnd 10:** *K2tog* around, ending with k1 (0, 0, 1, 0, 0).

Cut yarn and draw end through rem sts; tighten.

Weave in all ends neatly on WS.

**FINISHING**
Block cap by covering it with a damp towel; leave until completely dry.

Optional: Securely attach a pom-pom to top of cap.

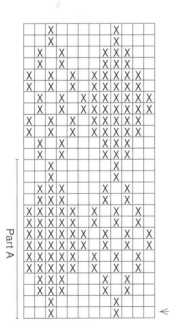

Part A

← begin here

☐ Knit on RS, purl on WS

☒ Purl on RS, knit on WS

# Easy Mittens

Nice and easy mittens with a delightful garter-stitch detail.

## Level 1

**Sizes:** 0–3 (3–6, 9–12 months, 1–2, 3–6, 7–10 years)

**MATERIALS**

**Yarn:** Sandnes Garn KlompeLompe Merinoull [CYCA #3 – DK, light worsted, 100% Merino wool, 114 yd (104 m) / 50 g]

**YARN COLORS AND AMOUNTS:**
Putty 1013: 50 (50, 50, 50, 50, 100) g

**Needles:** U.S. sizes 2.5 and 4 (3 and 3.5 mm): sets of 5 dpn; optional: 32 in (80 cm) circular for magic loop

**Notions:** 2 buttons for mittens with button flaps

**Gauge:** 22 sts on larger size needles = 4 in (10 cm).

Adjust needle size to obtain correct gauge if necessary.

-------------------------------------------------

With larger size dpn, CO 24 (28, 28, 30, 34, 36) sts. Divide sts onto 4 dpn and join.

Knit around in k1, p1 ribbing for 14 rnds.

Knit 1 rnd.

Knit 1 rnd, increasing 6 (8, 8, 6, 8, 6) sts evenly spaced around = 30 (36, 36, 36, 42, 42) sts.

Continue in stockinette until stockinette section measures 2¼ (2½, 3, 3½, 4¼, 5¼) in [5.5 (6.5, 7.5, 9, 11, 13) cm]. *At the same time*, for sizes 9–12 months (1–2, 3–6, 7–10 years), when stockinette section measures 1 (1¼, 1¼, 1⅜) in 2.5 (3, 3, 3.5) cm], make a thumbhole:

**RIGHT MITTEN**

K1, and then, with smooth contrast-color waste yarn, k- (–, 6, 6, 7, 7), slide the – (–, 6, 6, 7, 7) sts back to left needle and knit again with working yarn, knit to end of rnd.

**LEFT MITTEN**

K- (–, 11, 11, 13, 13), and then, with smooth contrast-color waste yarn, k- (–, 6, 6, 7, 7), slide the – (–, 6, 6, 7, 7) sts back to left needle and knit again with working yarn, knit to end of rnd.

After thumbhole, continue in stockinette to hand measurements specified above.

**SHAPE TOP:**

**Decrease Rnd 1:** *K4, k2tog*; rep * to * around.
Knit 1 rnd.

**Decrease Rnd 2:** *K3, k2tog*; rep * to * around.
Knit 1 rnd.

**Decrease Rnd 3:** *K2, k2tog*; rep * to * around.
Knit 1 rnd.

**Decrease Rnd 4:** *K1, k2tog*; rep * to * around.

**Decrease Rnd 5:** *K2tog*; rep * to * around.

Cut yarn and draw end through rem sts; tighten.

On the four largest sizes, work thumb with larger size dpn: Insert one dpn into the 6 (6, 7, 7) sts below waste yarn and a second dpn into the 6 (6, 7, 7) sts above waste yarn. Care-

fully remove waste yarn. Work around in stockinette for 1⅜ (1½, 2, 2¼) in [3.5 (4, 5, 6) cm. K2tog around. Cut yarn and draw end through rem sts; tighten.

### VERSION WITH BOW-TIE:
With smaller size dpn, pick up and knit 6 sts on side of mitten, 2 sts on garter st and 4 sts on stockinette.

Knit in garter st for 2¾ in (7 cm). Decrease on every other row as follows:

K2tog, knit to end of row.

Decrease the same way on every other row until 2 sts rem. On next row, cut yarn and draw end through rem 2 sts; tighten.

Make a strip the same way on opposite side of mitten. Tie the two strips together into a bow.

### VERSION WITH BUTTON FLAPS:
With smaller size dpn, pick up and knit 5 sts on thumb side of mitten, 2 sts on garter st and 3 sts on stockinette. Knit 10 (12, 12, 12, 14, 14) garter ridges (1 ridge = 2 knit rows). BO knitwise. Sew on a button, stitching through both flap and back of hand on mitten. Make a flap the same way on second mitten.

### FINISHING
Weave in all ends neatly.

Block mittens by covering them with a damp towel; leave until completely dry.

# Nerigjønå Cowl

When we wanted to go down to the local country store, we called the road Nerigjønå ("the down road"). This cowl was named for that rural road we frequently strolled on, and we still walk on it every day. The cowl has a fine-textured pattern and is fun to knit.

*Level 2*

---

**Sizes:** 6–12 months (1–2, 3–6, 7–10 years, women's)

**MATERIALS**
**Yarn:** Sandnes Garn KlompeLompe Merinoull [CYCA #3 – DK, light worsted, 100% Merino wool, 114 yd (104 m) / 50 g]

**YARN COLORS AND AMOUNTS:**
Blue-Green 6571: 50 (50, 100, 150, 200) g

**Needles:** U.S. size 4 (3.5 mm): 16 or 24 in (40 or 60 cm) circular

**Gauge:** 22 sts = 4 in (10 cm).

Adjust needle size to obtain correct gauge if necessary.

---

The cowl is worked in the round.

With circular, CO 80 (90, 100, 110, 120) sts. Join, being careful not to twist cast-on row; pm for beginning of rnd.

Work around following chart until cowl measures approx. 5¼ (6, 8¾, 11, 13½) in [13 (15, 22, 28, 34) cm].

BO knitwise.

**FINISHING**
Weave in all ends neatly on WS.

Block cowl by covering it with a damp towel; leave until completely dry.

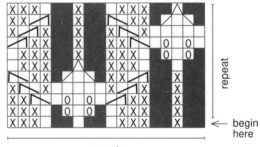

| | |
|---|---|
| ■ | no stitch |
| □ | knit |
| X | purl |
| O | yarnover |
| ╱ | k2tog |
| ╲ | sl 1, k1, psso |
| ◿ | sl 1, k2tog, psso |
| ╱ | knit 2nd st on left needle in front of 1st st, do not drop st off needle, purl 1st st; slip both sts off left needle |
| ╲ | purl 2nd st on left needle behind 1st st, do not drop st off needle, knit 1st st; slip both sts off left needle |

# Nerigjønå Cap

*Level 2*

**Sizes:** 0–1 (3, 6–9 months (1–2, 3–6, 7–10 years)

**MATERIALS**

**Yarn:** Sandnes Garn KlompeLompe Merinoull [CYCA #3 – DK, light worsted, 100% Merino wool, 114 yd (104 m) / 50 g]

**YARN COLORS AND AMOUNTS:**
Dark Gray-Blue 6061: 50 (50, 50, 50, 100, 100) g

**Needles:** U.S. sizes 2.5 and 4 (3 and 3.5 mm): 16 in (40 cm) circulars + set of 5 dpn (larger size); optional: 32 in (80 cm) circulars for magic loop

**Notions:** Optional: faux fur pom-pom

**Gauge:** 22 sts on larger size needles = 4 in (10 cm).

Adjust needle size to obtain correct gauge if necessary.

With smaller size circular, CO 68 (70, 76, 80, 84, 88) sts. Join, being careful not to twist cast-on row; pm for beginning of rnd.

Work 8 (8, 10, 10, 12, 12) rnds k1, p1 ribbing.

Change to larger size circular, Knit 1 rnd, increasing 2 (0, 4, 10, 6, 12) sts evenly spaced around = 70 (70, 80, 90, 90, 100) sts.

Work following chart.

After completing charted rows, continue in pattern: *K2, p7, k1*; rep * to * around.

When cap measures 4 (4¼, 5¼, 5¾, 6¼, 7) in [10 (11, 13, 14.5, 16, 18) cm], begin shaping crown (change to dpn when sts no longer fit around circular).

**Decrease Rnd 1:** *K2, p6, k2tog*; rep * to * around.
Work 2 rnds as: *K2, p6, k1*; rep * to * around.

**Decrease Rnd 2:** *K1, sl 1, k1, psso, p5, k1*; rep * to * around.
Work 2 rnds as: *K2, p5, k1*; rep * to * around.

**Decrease Rnd 3:** *K2, p4, k2tog*; rep * to * around.
Work 2 rnds as: *K2, p4, k1*; rep * to * around.

**Decrease Rnd 4:** *K1, sl 1, k1, psso, p3, k1*; rep * to * around.
Work 2 rnds as: *K2, p3, k1*; rep * to * around.

**Decrease Rnd 5:** *K2, p2, k2tog*; rep * to * around.
Work 1 rnd as: *K2, p2, k1*; rep * to * around.

**Decrease Rnd 6:** *K1, sl 1, k1, psso, p1, k1*; rep * to * around.
Work 1 rnd as: *K2, p1, k1*; rep * to * around.

**Decrease Rnd 7:** *K2, k2tog*; rep * to * around.
Knit 1 rnd.

**Decrease Rnd 8:** *K1, k2tog*; rep * to * around.

**Decrease Rnd 9:** *K2tog* around.

**FINISHING**

Cut yarn and draw end through rem sts; tighten.

Weave in all ends neatly on WS.

Block cap by covering it with a damp towel; leave until completely dry.

Optional: Securely attach a pom-pom to top of cap.

If you want a baggier version of this cap, you can make a larger size as we've done for the cap in the photo opposite.

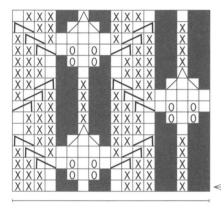

repeat

begin here

■ no stitch

☐ knit

☒ purl

⃞0 yarnover

⧄ k2tog

⟍ sl 1, k1, psso

⟁ sl 1, k2tog, psso

⧄ knit 2nd st on left needle in front of 1st st, do not drop st off needle, purl 1st st; slip both sts off left needle

⧅ purl 2nd st on left needle behind 1st st, do not drop st off needle, knit 1st st; slip both sts off left needle

# Wing Dress

A lovely dress for the winter season, with a full swing skirt and long sleeves. To top it off, there are fine wings on the sleeves and wooden buttons down the front neck placket.

*Level 3*

**Sizes:** 6–9 months (1, 2, 4, 6, 8, 10 years)

**FINISHED MEASUREMENTS**
Chest: Approx. 20 (21, 22¾, 23¾, 25¼, 26, 26) in [51 (53, 58, 60, 64, 66, 67.5) cm]

Length: Approx. 15¾ (18½, 19¼, 20½, 22½, 25¼, 26) in [40 (47, 49, 52, 57, 64, 66) cm]

**MATERIALS**
**Yarn:** Sandnes Garn KlompeLompe Merinoull [CYCA #3 – DK, light worsted, 100% Merino wool, 114 yd (104 m) / 50 g]

Sandnes Garn KlompeLompe Tynn Merinoull (fine Merino wool) [CYCA #1 – fingering, 100% Merino wool, 191 yd (175 m) / 50 g]

**YARN COLORS AND AMOUNTS:**
Merinoull Blue-Petroleum 7251: 200 (250, 300, 300, 350, 350, 400) g

Tynn Merinoull Blue-Petroleum 7251: 100 (100, 100, 150, 150, 150, 150) g

**Needles:** U.S. sizes 1.5, 2.5, and 4 (2.5, 3, and 3.5 mm): 16 and 32 in (40 and 80 cm) circulars and sets of 5 dpn in 2 smaller sizes

**Notions:** 3 (3, 3, 4, 4, 4, 4) buttons

**Gauge:** 22 sts on U.S. 4 (3.5 mm) needles and 27 sts on U.S. 2.5 (3 mm) needles = 4 in (10 cm).

Adjust needle sizes to obtain correct gauge if necessary.

The dress is worked from the bottom up, with the beginning of the round at the side.

With Merinoull and U.S. 4 (3.5 mm) circular, CO 260 (300, 320, 320, 330, 330, 340) sts.

Join, being careful not to twist cast-on row; pm for beginning of rnd. Purl 1 rnd, knit 1 rnd, purl 1 rnd.

Knit around for 3¼ (3½, 4, 4¾, 4¾, 5½, 6) in [8 (9, 10, 12, 12, 14, 15) cm]. On next rnd, decrease – (40, 40, 40, 40, 40, 40) sts evenly spaced around = 260 (260, 280, 280, 290, 290, 300) sts rem.

Knit around for 2½ (2¾, 3¼, 3½, 3½, 4, 4) in [6 (7, 8, 9, 9, 10, 10) cm]. On next rnd, decrease 40 (40, 40, 40, 40, 40, 40) sts evenly spaced around = 220 (220, 240, 240, 250, 250, 260) sts rem.

Knit around for 1½ (2, 2, 2¼, 3¼, 4, 4) in [4 (5, 5, 5.5, 8, 10, 10) cm]. On next rnd, decrease 40 (40, 40, 40, 40, 40, 40) sts evenly spaced around = 180 (180, 200, 200, 210, 210, 220) sts rem.

Knit around for 1½ (2, 2, 2¼, 2¼, 2½, 2½) in [4 (5, 5, 5.5, 5.5, 6, 6) cm]. On next rnd, decrease 40 (40, 40, 40, 40, 40, 40) sts evenly spaced around = 140 (140, 160, 160, 170, 170, 180) sts rem.

Knit around for 1½ (2, 2, 2¼, 2¼, 2½, 2½) in [4 (5, 5, 5.5, 5.5, 6, 6) cm]. On next rnd, decrease 28 (20, 40, 28, 30, 22, 28) sts evenly spaced around = 112 (120, 120, 132, 140, 148, 152) sts rem.

Purl 1 rnd.

Knit 1 rnd, and, *at the same time*, bind off sts for placket: K26 (28, 28, 31, 33, 35, 36), BO 4 sts, knit to end of rnd. Slip the 26 (28, 28, 31, 33, 35, 36) front sts up to placket onto right needle. The row now begins at this point, and, you will also begin working back and forth.

Purl 1 rnd.

Knit 1 rnd, and, *at the same time*, bind off sts for placket: K26 (28, 28, 31, 33, 35, 36), BO 4 sts, knit to end of rnd. Slip the 26 (28, 28, 31, 33, 35, 36) front sts up to placket onto right needle. The row now begins at this point, and, you will also begin working back and forth.

Change to U.S. 2.5 (3 mm) circular and Tynn Merinoull. Knit 1 row on RS, increasing 30 (28, 40, 34, 38, 34, 34) sts evenly spaced across = 138 (144, 156, 162, 174, 178, 182) sts. Work back and forth in stockinette for ¾ (¾, ¾, 1¼, 1¼, 1½, 2) in [2 (2, 2, 3, 3, 4, 5) cm].

Now divide body for front and back: K24 (25, 28, 29, 32, 33, 34), BO 19 (20, 20, 21, 22, 22, 22) sts, k52 (54, 60, 62, 66, 68, 70), BO 19 (20, 20, 21, 22, 22, 22) sts, k24 (25, 28, 29, 32, 33, 34).

**LEFT FRONT**
The first row = WS.

Purl 1 row.

**Next Row:** K1, k2tog, knit to end of row.

Rep these two rows a total of 4 times = 20 (21, 24, 25, 28, 29, 30) sts rem.

Continue back and forth in stockinette until front measures 3½ (3½, 4, 4, 4¼, 4¼, 4¾) in [9 (9, 10, 10, 11, 11, 12) cm] *above purl round.*

**Next Row (WS):** With an extra needle, purl the first 8 (8, 10, 10, 12, 12, 12) sts.

The rem 12 (13, 14, 15, 16, 17, 18) sts will be worked separately for the shoulder. P12 (13, 14, 15, 16, 17, 18).

**Next Row:** Knit until 3 sts rem, k2tog, k1.

Turn and purl across.

Rep these two rows a total of 4 times. Continue in stockinette for 1¼ (1¼, 1¼, 1¼, 1½, 1½, 1½) in [3 (3, 3, 3, 4, 4, 4) cm].

**Next Row (RS):** BO knitwise.

**RIGHT FRONT**
The first row = WS.

Purl 1 row.

**Next Row:** Knit until 3 sts rem, sl 1, k1, psso, k1.

Rep these two rows a total of 4 times = 20 (21, 24, 25, 28, 29, 30) sts rem.

Continue back and forth in stockinette until front measures 3½ (3½, 4, 4, 4¼, 4¼, 4¾) in [9 (9, 10, 10, 11, 11, 12) cm] *above purl round.*

**Next Row (WS):** With an extra needle, purl the last 8 (8, 10, 10, 12, 12, 12) sts. Cut yarn and re-attach to work the rem 12 (13, 14, 15, 16, 17, 18) sts for shoulder.

**Next Row:** K1, k2tog, knit to end of row.

Turn and purl across.

Rep these two rows a total of 4 times. Continue in stockinette for 1¼ (1¼, 1¼, 1¼, 1½, 1½, 1½) in [3 (3, 3, 3, 4, 4, 4) cm].

**Next Row (RS):** BO knitwise.

**BACK**
The first row = WS. Purl 1 row.

**Next Row:** K1, k2tog, knit until 3 sts rem, sl 1, k1, psso, k1.

Rep these two rows a total of 4 times.

Continue back and forth in stockinette without decreasing until back measures 4¼ (4¼, 4¾, 4¾, 5¼, 5¼, 5½) in [11 (11, 12, 12, 13, 13, 14) cm] *above purl round.*

**Next Row (WS):** With an extra needle, purl the first 32 (33, 38, 39, 42, 43, 44) sts and purl the last 12 (13, 14, 15, 16, 17, 18) sts for left strap.

**Next Row:** Knit until 3 sts rem, k2tog, k1.

Turn and purl across.

Rep these two rows a total of 4 times.

**Next Row (RS):** BO knitwise.

Beginning on RS, work the first 12 (13, 14, 15, 16, 17, 18 sts on extra needle for right shoulder as follows:

K1, k2tog, knit to end of row.

**Next Row (WS):** Purl across.

Rep these two rows a total of 4 times.

**Next Row (RS):** BO knitwise.

Seam shoulders.

### BUTTONHOLE BAND
With Tynn Merinoull and U.S. 1.5 (2.5 mm) needles, pick up and knit sts on right side of placket.

Pick up and knit 1 st each of next 3 sts, skip 4th st along placket edge. Work 8 rows in k1, p1 ribbing, *but*, on the 3rd row, make 2 (2, 2, 3, 3, 3, 3) buttonholes evenly spaced on band: for each buttonhole, BO 2 sts and CO 2 sts over gap on next row.

**Note:** The 3rd (3rd, 3rd, 4th, 4th, 4th, 4th) buttonhole will be made in the neckband.

Make a band on the left side of placket the same way, omitting buttonholes.

### NECKBAND RIBBING
With Tynn Merinoull and U.S. 1.5 (2.5 mm) circular, pick up and knit 6 sts along end of button band, k8 (8, 10, 10, 12, 12, 12) from extra needle, pick up and knit 22 (22, 22, 22, 26, 26, 26) sts along shoulder, k20 (20, 24, 24, 26, 26, 26) held sts, pick up and knit 22 (22, 22, 22, 26, 26, 26) sts along shoulder, k8 (8, 10, 10, 12, 12, 12) from extra needle, pick up and knit 6 sts along end of button band = 92 (92, 100, 100, 114, 114, 114) sts total.

Work 8 rows in k1, p1 ribbing, *but*, on the 3rd row, make a buttonhole: Work in ribbing as est until 5 sts rem, BO 2 sts, work 3 sts in ribbing. On next row, CO 2 sts over gap. Complete ribbing rows and BO in ribbing.

### SLEEVES
With Tynn Merinoull and U.S. 2.5 (3 mm) circular, beginning at center of underarm, pick up and knit 85 (85, 89, 89, 93, 93, 97) sts around armhole. Pm for beginning of rnd. Knit 1 rnd.

Now work short rows back and forth.

**Note:** Make a yo after every turn and, when you later come to it, knit/purl yo tog with following st.

**Sizes 6–9 months and 1 year:** K67; turn; p51; turn. K52; turn; p53; turn. K54; turn; p55; turn. K56; turn; p57; turn. K58, k2tog; turn; p60, p2tog; turn. K62, k2tog; turn; p64, p2tog; turn. K66, k2tog; turn; p68, p2tog; turn. K70, k2tog; turn; p72, p2tog; turn. K75. You should now be back at beginning of row = 77 sts.

**Sizes 2 and 4 years:** K71; turn; p55; turn. K56; turn; p57; turn. K58; turn; p59; turn. K60; turn; p61; turn. K62, k2tog; turn; p64, p2tog; turn. K66, k2tog; turn; p68, p2tog; turn. K70, k2tog; turn; p72, p2tog; turn. K74, k2tog; turn; p76, p2tog; turn. K79. You should now be back at beginning of row = 81 sts.

**Sizes 6 and 8 years:** K75; turn; p59; turn. K60; turn; p61; turn. K62; turn; p63; turn. K64; turn; p65; turn. K66, k2tog; turn; p68, p2tog; turn. K70, k2tog; turn; p72, p2tog; turn. K74, k2tog; turn; p76, p2tog; turn. K78, k2tog; turn; p80, p2tog; turn. K83. You should now be back at beginning of row = 85 sts.

**Sizes 10 years:** K79; turn; p63; turn. K64; turn; p65; turn. K66; turn; p67; turn. K68; turn; p69; turn. K70, k2tog; turn; p72, p2tog; turn. K74, k2tog; turn; p76, p2tog; turn. K78, k2tog; turn; p80, p2tog; turn. K82, k2tog; turn; p84, p2tog; turn. K87. You should now be back at beginning of row = 89 sts.

**ALL SIZES** (*BEGIN WORKING IN THE ROUND*):
Knit 1 rnd. Knit next rnd, decreasing 8 sts evenly spaced around. Knit 3 rnds. Knit 1 rnd, decreasing 8 sts evenly spaced around = 61 (61, 65, 65, 69, 69, 73) sts rem.

Continue around in stockinette until sleeve measures 6¾ (7½, 9½, 10¾, 11¾, 13, 14¼) in [17 (19, 24, 27, 30, 33, 36) cm], **but**, after ⅝ in (1.5 cm), decrease as follows: K1, k2tog, knit until 3 sts rem, sl 1, k1, psso, k1. Rep this decrease rnd every ¾ (¾, 1, 1¼, 1¼, 1¼, 1¼) in [2 (2, 2.5, 3, 3, 3, 3) cm] until 45 (45, 49, 49, 51, 51, 51) sts rem. Knit 1 rnd, decreasing 1 st (center of underarm).

Change to dpn U.S. 1.5 (2.5 mm). Work around in k1, p1 ribbing for 1⅜ (1⅜, 1⅜, 1½, 1½, 2, 2) in [3.5 (3.5, 3.5, 4, 4, 5, 5) cm]. On last rnd, BO in ribbing.

Make second sleeve the same way.

**WINGS (SAME ON EACH SLEEVE )**
**Note:** Wings are worked with U.S. 2.5 (3 mm) circular and Tynn Merinull.

After each turn, slip first st, tugging yarn slightly.

Now you will pick up and knit sts in a straight line up from the lower edge of front stockinette section, around and down to lower edge of back stockinette section. Begin left wing on front and right wing on back. Pick up and knit sts in last row before shoulders. Pick up 1 st in each st on yoke.

Knit 2 rows.

K18 (18, 20, 20, 24, 24, 26), continue knitting, with M1 after every 6th st until 18 (18, 20, 20, 24, 24, 26) sts rem; turn.

Knit until 18 (18, 20, 20, 24, 24, 26) sts rem; turn.

Knit until 5 sts before last turn; turn.

Knit until 5 sts before last turn; turn.

Knit with M1 after every 7th st until 5 sts before last turn; turn.

Knit until 5 sts before last turn; turn.

Knit to end of row.

Knit across all sts.

BO knitwise.

Sew down tips of wings to dress.

**FINISHING**
Sew down lower end of each placket band to dress.

Weave in all ends neatly on WS.

Sew on buttons.

Block by covering dress with a damp towel and leaving it until completely dry.

# Wing Dress for Dolls

As everyone knows, the doll baby must have
the same dress as the doll's mother.

*Level 3*

---

**Sizes:** One size (Baby Born doll)

**MATERIALS**

**Yarn:** Sandnes Garn KlompeLompe Tynn Merinoull (fine Merino wool) [CYCA #1 – fingering, 100% Merino wool, 191 yd (175 m) / 50 g]

**YARN COLORS AND AMOUNTS:**
Putty 1013 or Powder Rose 4032: 100 g

**Needles:** U.S. sizes 1.5 and 2.5 (2.5 and 3 mm): 16 and 32 in (40 and 80 cm) circulars and sets of 5 dpn

**Notions:** 3 buttons

**Gauge:** 27 sts on larger size needles = 4 in (10 cm).

Adjust needle sizes to obtain correct gauge if necessary.

---

The dress is worked from the bottom up, with the beginning of the round at the side.

With larger size circular, CO 146 sts.

Join, being careful not to twist cast-on row; pm for beginning of rnd. Purl 1 rnd, knit 1 rnd, purl 1 rnd.

Knit around for 1½ in (4 cm) On next rnd, decrease 20 sts evenly spaced around = 126 sts rem.

Knit around for 1½ in (4 cm) On next rnd, decrease 20 sts evenly spaced around = 106 sts rem.

Knit around for 1½ in (4 cm) On next rnd, decrease 20 sts evenly spaced around = 86 sts rem.

Purl 1 rnd.

Knit 1 rnd, and, *at the same time*, bind off sts for placket: K19, BO 4 sts, knit to end of rnd.

Slip the 19 front sts up to placket onto right needle. The row now begins at this point, and, you will also work back and forth.

Work back and forth in stockinette for ⅜ in (1) cm.

Now divide body for front and back: K15, BO 10 sts, k32, BO 10 sts, k15.

**LEFT FRONT**
The first row = WS.

Purl 1 row.

**Next Row:** K1, k2tog, knit to end of row.

Rep these two rows a total of 2 times = 13 sts rem.

Continue back and forth in stockinette until front measures 1½ in (4 cm) *above purl round*.

**Next Row (WS):** With an extra needle, purl the first 5 sts.

The rem 8 sts will be worked separately for the shoulder. P8.

**Next Row:** Knit until 3 sts rem, k2tog, k1.

Turn and purl across.

Rep these two rows a total of 2 times. Continue in stockinette for ¾ in (2 cm).

**Next Row (RS):** BO knitwise.

**RIGHT FRONT**
The first row = WS.

Purl 1 row.

**Next Row:** Knit until 3 sts rem, sl 1, k1, psso, k1.

Rep these two rows a total of 2 times = 13 sts rem.

Continue back and forth in stockinette until front measures 1½ (4 cm) *above purl round*.

**Next Row (WS):** With an extra needle, purl the last 5 sts. Cut yarn and re-attach to work the rem 8 sts for shoulder.

**Next Row:** K1, k2tog, knit to end of row.

Turn and purl across.

Rep these two rows a total of 2 times. Continue in stockinette for ¾ in (2 cm).

**Next Row (RS):** BO knitwise.

**BACK**
The first row = WS. Purl 1 row.

**Next Row:** K1, k2tog, knit until 3 sts rem, sl 1, k1, psso, k1.

Rep these two rows a total of 2 times.

Continue back and forth in stockinette without decreasing until back measures 2½ in (6 cm) *above purl round*.

**Next Row (WS):** With an extra needle, purl the first 20 sts and purl the last 8 sts for left strap.

**Next Row:** Knit until 3 sts rem, k2tog, k1.

Turn and purl across.

Rep these two rows a total of 2 times.

**Next Row (RS):** BO knitwise.

Beginning on RS, work the first 8 sts on extra needle for right shoulder as follows:

K1, k2tog, knit to end of row.

**Next Row (WS):** Purl across.

Rep these two rows a total of 2 times.

**Next Row (RS):** BO knitwise.

Seam shoulders.

**BUTTONHOLE BAND**
With Tynn Merinoull and smaller size needles, pick up and knit sts on right side of placket.

Pick up and knit 1 st each of next 3 sts, skip 4th st along placket edge. Work 8 rows in k1, p1 ribbing, *but*, on the 3rd row, make 2 buttonholes evenly spaced on band: for each buttonhole, BO 2 sts and CO 2 sts over gap on next row.

**Note:** The 3rd buttonhole will be made in the neckband.

Make a band on the left side of placket the same way, omitting buttonholes.

**NECKBAND RIBBING**
With smaller size circular, pick up and knit 6 sts along end of button band, k5 from extra needle, pick up and knit 17 sts along shoulder, k12 held sts, pick up and knit 17 sts along shoulder, k5 from extra needle, pick up and knit 6 sts along end of button band = 68 sts total.

Work 6 rows in k1, p1 ribbing, *but*, on the 2nd row, make a buttonhole: Rib 3, BO 2 sts, work in ribbing to end of row. On next row, CO 2 sts over gap. Complete ribbing rows and BO in ribbing.

## SLEEVES

With larger size circular, beginning at center of underarm, pick up and knit 45 sts around armhole. Pm for beginning of rnd. Knit 1 rnd.

Now work short rows back and forth (yo after every turn and, when you later come to it, knit yo tog with following st):

K37; turn, p29; turn. K30; turn, p31; turn. K32; turn, p33; turn. K34, k2tog; turn, p36, p2tog; turn. K38, k2tog; turn, p40, p2tog; turn. Knit to end of row = 41 sts.

*Begin working in the round.*

Knit 1 rnd. Knit next rnd, decreasing 3 sts evenly spaced around = 38 sts rem.

Continue around in stockinette until sleeve measures 3¼ in (8 cm, *but*, after 1¼ in (3 cm), decrease as follows: K1, k2tog, knit until 3 sts rem, sl 1, k1, psso, k1. Rep this decrease rnd every ¾ in (2 cm) until 32 sts rem.

Change to smaller size dpn. Work 8 rnds in k1, p1 ribbing. On last rnd, BO in ribbing.

Make second sleeve the same way.

## WINGS (SAME ON EACH SLEEVE )

**Note:** Wings are worked with larger size circular.

After each turn, slip first st, tugging yarn slightly.

Now you will pick up and knit sts in a straight line up from the lower edge of front stockinette section, around and then down to lower edge of back stockinette section. Begin left wing on front and right wing on back. Pick up and knit sts in last row before shoulders. Pick up 1 st in each st on yoke.

Knit 2 rows.

K4, continue knitting, with M1 after every 6th st until 4 sts rem; turn.

Knit until 4 sts rem; turn.

Knit until 5 sts before last turn; turn.

Knit until 5 sts before last turn; turn.

Knit with M1 after every 7th st until 5 sts before last turn; turn.

Knit until 5 sts before last turn; turn.

Knit to end of row.

Knit across all sts.

BO knitwise.

Sew down tips of wings to dress.

## FINISHING

Sew down lower end of each placket band to dress.

Weave in all ends neatly on WS.

Sew on buttons.

Block by covering dress with a damp towel and leaving it until completely dry.

# Dinosaur Onesie

We designed a dinosaur cardigan for our book *Summer Knitting for Little Sweethearts.* It became the littlest one's favorite, so we wanted to also feature the dinosaur pattern in this book. Here's a sweet onesie with button details at the neck and knitted with fine yarn.

*Level 2*

**Sizes:** 1–3 months (6–9 months, 1, 2 years)

**FINISHED MEASUREMENTS**
Chest: Approx. 18¾ (19¾, 21¾, 23¼) in [47.5 (50, 55, 59) cm]

Total Length: Approx. 13¾ (15, 17¼, 19¼) in [35 (38, 44, 49) cm]

**MATERIALS**
**Yarn:** Sandnes Garn KlompeLompe Tynn Merinoull (fine Merino wool) [CYCA #1 – fingering, 100% Merino wool, 191 yd (175 m) / 50 g]

**YARN COLORS AND AMOUNTS:**
Color A: Blue-Petroleum 7251: 150 (150, 150, 200) g

Color B: Gray-Brown 2652: 50 (50, 50, 50) g

**Needles:** U.S. sizes 1.5 and 2.5 (2.5 and 3 mm): 16 and 24 in (40 and 60 cm) circulars and sets of 5 dpn

**Notions:** 6 (6, 6, 6) buttons

**Gauge:** 27 sts on larger size needles = 4 in (10 cm).

Adjust needle size to obtain correct gauge if necessary.

The onesie is worked from the top down, beginning back and forth on a circular.

**BODY**
With smaller size circular and color A, CO 95 (99, 99, 103) sts. Work 8 rows back and forth in k1, p1 ribbing except for the first 5 and last 5 sts which are always knitted in garter st.

On the 4th row, make a buttonhole as follows: Work as est until 4 st rem, BO 2 sts, k2. On the next row, CO 2 new sts over the gap.

Change to larger size circular.

**Note:** Do not increase in the garter st bands unless specifically instructed to do so.

Knit 1 rnd, increasing 44 (48, 48, 52) sts evenly spaced across = 139 (147, 147, 155) sts.

Work 5 (5, 7, 9) rows in stockinette, maintaining the 5 garter sts at beginning and end of row. On the 4th (4th, 6th, 8th) row, make a buttonhole as before. Knit 1 row, increasing 22 (24, 34, 36) sts evenly spaced across = 161 (171, 181, 191) sts.

Work 3 (5, 7, 7) rows in stockinette, still maintaining the garter sts. Knit 1 row, increasing 20 (26, 32, 38) sts evenly spaced across = 181 (197, 213, 229) sts.

Purl 1 row. On next row (RS), BO first 5 sts and begin knitting in the round = 176 (192, 208, 224) sts.

Now work following chart.

After completing charted rows, you should have 198 (216, 234, 252) sts.

Knit 1 rnd, adjusting stitch count to 212 (220, 240, 252) sts.

Knit 0 (0, 0, 4) rnds with color A.

Place sleeve sts onto holders as follows: Place the next 49 (49, 53, 53) sts on a holder, CO 7 sts for underarm, k57 (61, 67, 73), place next 49 (49, 53, 53) sts on a holder, CO 7 sts for underarm, k57 (61, 67, 73).

## FRONT AND BACK
There should now be 128 (136, 148, 160) sts for body.

Continue around in stockinette until body measures 11½ (12¾, 14½, 15¾) in [29 (32, 37, 40) cm]. Now divide for front and back: K62 (66, 70, 78), BO 22 (22, 24, 26) sts, k32 (36, 40, 40), BO 22 (22, 24, 26) sts. You've now bound off past beginning of rnd and divided body into front and back.

## BACK
Work back separately, back and forth = 52 (56, 60, 68) sts.

The first row = RS. On every RS row, decrease 1 st at each side with k2tog at beginning of row and k2tog at end of row. Continue decreasing until 26 (28, 30, 30) sts rem. Place rem sts on a holder and set aside while you knit front.

## FRONT
Work as for back over the 32 (36, 40, 40) sts, decreasing as for back until 26 (28, 30, 30) sts rem. Continue without decreasing until front is ¾ in (2 cm) shorter than back.

Place rem sts on a holder and set aside while you work ribbing around legs.

With smaller size circular, pick up and knit 1 st in each st around, skipping every 4th st. Work 6 rnds in k1, p1 ribbing, and BO in ribbing on last rnd. Work around second leg the same way.

## BUTTON BANDS ON CROTCH:
With smaller size needles and color A, pick up and knit 4 sts on end of ribbing around leg, knit held sts, pick up and knit 4 sts on end of opposite ribbed leg band. Work in k1, p1 ribbing for 6 rows. On front band, make 4 buttonholes evenly spaced across on 3rd row (buttonhole: k2tog, yo).

## SLEEVES
With larger size dpn and color A, CO 4 sts, k49 (49, 53, 53) held sts, CO 3 sts. The first st is a marked st at center of underarm and should be purled on every rnd. Work around in stockinette until sleeve is ⅝ in (1.5 cm) long. Begin shaping sleeve:

P1 (marked st), k2tog, knit until 2 sts rem, sl 1, k1, psso. Decrease the same way every ⅝ (¾, ¾, 1¼) in [1.5 (2, 2, 3) cm] until 40 (42, 42, 44) sts rem and sleeve measures 4¾ (6¼, 7, 9½) in [12 (16, 18, 24) cm].

Knit 1 rnd, decreasing 6 sts evenly spaced around.

Change to smaller size dpn and work 10 rnds k1, p1 ribbing; BO in ribbing on last rnd.

## FINISHING
Weave in all ends neatly on WS.

Stitch down short ends of back. Sew on buttons.

Block by covering onesie with a damp towel; leave until completely dry.

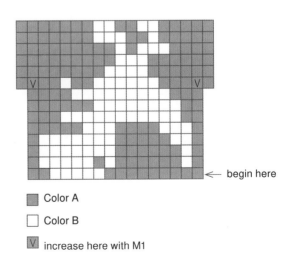

← begin here

■ Color A

☐ Color B

V increase here with M1

# Hubbabubba Cowl

A soft, beautiful cowl with a fancy texture.
Knitted on big needles, it's a quick project.

---

## Level 1

**Sizes:** 1–2 (3–6, 7–10) years

**MATERIALS**
**Yarn:** Sandnes Garn KlompeLompe Spøt [CYCA #3 – DK, light worsted, 40% Merino wool, 40% alpaca, 20% nylon, 147 yd (134 m) / 50 g]

**YARN COLORS AND AMOUNTS:**
Soft Purple 4331: 100 (100, 200) g

**Needles:** U.S. size 9 (5.5 mm): 16 in (40 cm) circular

**Gauge:** 16 sts with two strands of yarn held together = 4 in (10 cm).

Adjust needle size to obtain correct gauge if necessary.

---

With two strands of yarn held together, CO 64 (80, 96) sts. Join, being careful not to twist cast-on row; pm for beginning of rnd.

Work around in Bobble pattern. Don't forget to tighten the sts forming bobbles.

**BOBBLE PATTERN**
Knit 11 rnds.

**Bobble Rnd 1:** *K7, drop 1 st down 10 rows, knit the 10 strands together with the st below*; rep * to * around.

Knit 11 rnds.

**Bobble Rnd 2:** *K3, drop 1 st down 10 rows, knit the 10 strands together with the st below, k4*; rep * to * around.

Work a total of 4 (5, 7) bobble rnds.

Knit 1 rnd.

BO knitwise.

**FINISHING**
Weave in all ends neatly on WS. Block by covering cowl with a damp towel; leave until completely dry.

# Hubbabubba Cap

An easy cap with the same amusing texture
as the Hubbabubba cowl.

*Level 1*

**Sizes:** 6 months (1–2, 3–6, 7–10) years

**MATERIALS**
**Yarn:** Sandnes Garn KlompeLompe Merinoull [CYCA #3 –
DK, light worsted, 100% Merino wool, 114 yd (104 m) / 50 g]

**YARN COLORS AND AMOUNTS:**
Soft Purple 4331: 50 (50, 100, 100) g

**Needles:** U.S. sizes 2.5 and 4 (3 and 3.5 mm): 16 in (40 cm)
circulars and sets of 5 dpn

**Gauge:** 22 sts on larger size needles = 4 in (10 cm).

Adjust needle size to obtain correct gauge if necessary.

With smaller size circular, CO 80 (84, 88, 92) sts. Join, being
careful not to twist cast-on row; pm for beginning of rnd.
Work around in k1, p1 ribbing for 1¼ in (3 cm).

Change to larger size circular. Knit 1 rnd increasing 4 (6, 8,
10) sts evenly spaced around = 84 (90, 96, 102) sts. Work
around in stockinette for 1¼ in (3 cm).

Work around in Bobble pattern. Don't forget to tighten the
sts forming bobbles.

**BOBBLE PATTERN**
**Bobble Rnd 1:** *K5, drop 1 st down 6 rows, knit the 6 strands
together with the st below*; rep * to * around.

Knit 7 rnds.

**Bobble Rnd 2:** *K2, drop 1 st down 6 rows, knit the 6
strands together with the st below, k3*; rep * to * around.

Knit 7 rnds.

Work a total of 3 (3, 4, 4) bobble rnds.

Continue in stockinette until cap measures 5¼ (6, 6¾, 7½)
in [13 (15, 17, 19) cm].

Knit 1 rnd, decreasing 4 (2, 0, 6) sts evenly spaced around.

**SHAPE CROWN** (CHANGE TO DPN WHEN STS NO LONGER FIT AROUND CIRCULAR).
**Decrease Rnd 1:** *K6, k2tog*; rep * to * around.
Knit 2 rnds.

**Decrease Rnd 2:** *K5, k2tog*; rep * to * around.
Work 2 rnds.

**Decrease Rnd 3:** *K4, k2tog*; rep * to * around.
Work 2 rnds.

**Decrease Rnd 4:** *K3, k2tog*; rep * to * around.
Work 1 rnd, decreasing 0 (4, 0, 0) sts evenly spaced around.

**Decrease Rnd 5:** *K6, k2tog*; rep * to * around.

**Decrease Rnd 6:** *K5, k2tog*; rep * to * around.

**Decrease Rnd 7:** *K4, k2tog*; rep * to * around.

**Decrease Rnd 8:** *K3, k2tog*; rep * to * around.

**Decrease Rnd 9:** *K2, k2tog* around.

**Decrease Rnd 10:** *K2tog* around.

**FINISHING**
Cut yarn and draw end through rem sts; tighten.

Weave in all ends neatly on WS.

Block cap by covering it with a damp towel; leave until completely dry.

# Super-Easy Poncho

As the name implies, this is an unbelievably easy garment to make. It fits closely and is knitted in a delightful fiber blend yarn.

## Level 1

**Sizes:** 6 months (1, 2, 4, 6, 8, 10) years

**FINISHED MEASUREMENTS**
Total Length *from shoulder down*: 11 (13, 15, 16½, 18¼, 19¼, 20½) in [28 (33, 38, 42, 46, 49, 52) cm]

**MATERIALS**
**Yarn:** Sandnes Garn KlompeLompe Spøt [CYCA #3 – DK, light worsted, 40% Merino wool, 40% alpaca, 20% nylon, 147 yd (134 m) / 50 g]

**YARN COLORS AND AMOUNTS:**
Blue-Green 6871: 100 (150, 150, 150, 200, 200, 200) g

**Needles:** U.S. size 4 (3.5 mm): 24 in (60 cm) circular and set of 5 dpn

**Notions:** 6 (6, 6, 8, 8, 8, 8) buttons

**Gauge:** 22 sts = 4 in (10 cm).

Adjust needle size to obtain correct gauge if necessary.

The poncho begins at lower edge of front and is worked back and forth.

With circular, CO 56 (60, 64, 64, 68, 72, 78) sts. Work 6 rows in seed st (Row 1: *K1, p1*; rep * to * across. Subsequent rows: Work purl over knit and knit over purl.)

**Note:** On 3rd seed st row, make a buttonhole: Work 3 seed sts, BO 2 sts, work as est until 5 sts rem, BO 2 sts, 3 seed sts. On next row, CO 2 sts over each gap.

Work a total of 3 (3, 3, 4, 4, 4, 4) buttonholes on each side, spaced about 2 in (5 cm) apart.

Continue with the 6 sts outermost at each side in seed st and rem sts in stockinette. On next row, increase as follows: 6 seed sts, k1, M1, knit until 7 sts rem, M1, k1, 6 seed sts.

Increase the same way every ⅜ in (1 cm) a total of 5 (5, 6, 6, 6, 7, 7) times = 66 (70, 76, 76, 80, 86, 92) sts.

Pm at each side for later measurements.

Continue as est until piece measures 11 (13, 15, 16½, 18¼, 19¼, 20½) in [28 (33, 38, 42, 46, 49, 52) cm] in total.

**Shape neck:** Work 13 (15, 18, 16, 18, 20, 23) sts, BO 40 (40, 40, 44, 44, 46, 46) sts, work 13 (15, 18, 16, 18, 20, 23) sts (continuing seed on each side).

On next row, CO 40 (40, 40, 44, 44, 46, 46) sts over previous bind-off.

Now work back as for front down to side markers. Begin decreasing as follows:

6 seed sts, k1, k2tog, knit until 9 sts rem, k2tog, k1, 6 seed sts.

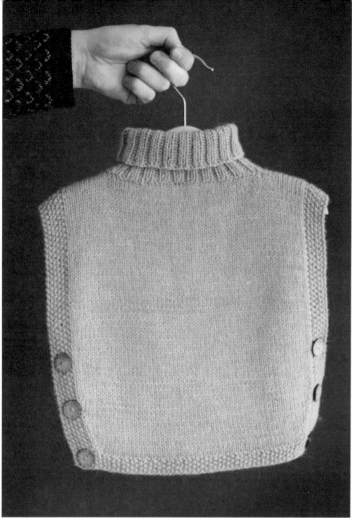

Color 6041

Decrease the same way every ⅜ in (1 cm) a total of 5 (5, 6, 6, 6, 7, 7) times = 56 (60, 64, 64, 68, 72, 78) sts.

Work 6 rows in seed st and then BO in seed st.

### NECKBAND
Pick up and knit 1 st in each st around neck = 80 (80, 80, 88, 88, 92, 92) sts total. Work around in k2, p2 ribbing for 4 (4, 4, 4, 4, 4¾, 4¾) in [10 (10, 10, 10, 10, 12, 12) cm]. BO in ribbing on last rnd.

### FINISHING
Weave in all ends neatly on WS. Sew on buttons. Block poncho by covering it with a damp towel; leave until completely dry.

# Lighthouse Pullover

We've revamped an old favorite, Lighthouse, as a pullover knitted with heavier yarn. It's a great choice for wearing on a cold winter day.

*Level 2*

**Sizes:** 6 months (1, 2, 4, 6, 8, 10) years

**FINISHED MEASUREMENTS**

Chest: Approx. 22¾ (22¾, 24½, 25¾, 27¼, 28¾, 31½) in [58 (58, 62, 65.5, 69, 73, 80) cm]

Total Length: Approx.13 (13½, 14¼, 15¾, 17, 19¼, 21¾) in [33 (34, 36, 40, 43, 49, 55) cm]

**MATERIALS**

**Yarn:** Sandnes Garn KlompeLompe Spøt [CYCA #3 – DK, light worsted, 40% Merino wool, 40% alpaca, 20% nylon, 147 yd (134 m) / 50 g]

**YARN COLORS AND AMOUNTS:**

Color A: Light Brown 2652: 150 (150, 150, 200, 200, 250, 300) g

Color B: Flax Blue 6051: 50 (50, 50, 50, 50, 50, 50) g

Color C: Light Flax Blue 6041: 50 (50, 50, 50, 50, 50, 50) g

Color D: Putty 1013: 50 (50, 50, 50, 50, 50, 50) g

**Needles:** U.S. sizes 2.5 and 4 (3 and 3.5 mm): 16 and 24 in (40 and 60 cm) circulars and set of 5 dpn; optional 32 in (80 cm) circulars for magic loop

**Gauge:** 22 sts = 4 in (10 cm).

Adjust needle size to obtain correct gauge if necessary.

The sweater begins at lower edge and is worked in the round on a circular needle.

With color A and smaller size circular, CO 128 (128, 136, 144, 152, 160, 176) sts. Join, being careful not to twist cast-on row; pm for beginning of rnd. Work around in k1, p1 ribbing for 8 (8, 10, 10, 10, 10, 12) rnds. Change to larger size circular. Knit 1 rnd. Work following chart A for all sizes except 6 months and 1 year.

After completing charted rows, continue in stockinette with color A only until body measures 8¼ (8¾, 9½, 10¼, 11, 13, 15) in [21 (22, 24, 26, 28, 33, 38) cm]. On next rnd, decrease as follows:

BO 6 sts, k58 (58, 62, 66, 70, 74, 82), BO 6 sts, k58 (58, 62, 66, 70, 74, 82).

Set body aside while you knit sleeves.

**SLEEVES**

With color A and smaller size dpn, CO 30 (32, 34, 36, 38, 40, 42) sts. Divide sts onto dpn and join; pm for beginning of rnd. Work around in k1, p1 ribbing for 8 (8, 10, 10, 10, 10, 12) rnds. Change to larger size dpn. Knit 1 rnd, increasing 2 (0, 6, 4, 2, 0 6) sts evenly spaced around = 32 (32, 40, 40, 40, 40, 48) sts. Work following chart A for all sizes except 6 months and 1 year.

After completing charted rows, continue in stockinette with color A only until sleeve measures 8 (8¾, 10¾, 12¾, 13½, 15, 16¼) in [20.5 (22.5, 27, 32, 34, 38, 41.5) cm].

**Note:** After working ⅜ in (1 cm) above ribbing, begin shaping sleeve: K1, M1, knit until 1 st rem, M1, k1.

Increase the same way every 1 (¾, 1¼, 1¼, 1, ¾, 1¼) in [2.5 (2, 3, 3, 2.5, 2, 3) cm] until there are 46 (48, 50, 54, 58, 64, 68) sts. On next rnd, BO the first 3 and last 3 sts.

Set first sleeve aside while you knit second sleeve the same way.

### YOKE

Arrange all pieces on same larger size circular, matching underarms = 196 (200, 212, 228, 244, 264, 288) sts total.

With color A, knit 0 (0, 0, 2, 4, 8, 10) rnds.

Knit 1 rnd, decreasing 4 (8, 8, 0, 16, 12, 24) sts evenly spaced around = 192 (192, 204, 228, 228, 252, 264) sts rem.

Knit 0 (0, 0, 6, 7, 6, 7) rnds.

Knit 0 (0, 0, 0, 0, 1, 1) rnd decreasing 0 (0, 0, 0, 10, 12, 12) sts evenly spaced around = 192 (192, 204, 228 228, 240, 252) sts rem.

52

Work following chart B.

After completing charted rows, 80 (80, 85, 95, 95, 100, 105) sts rem.

Knit 1 rnd with color A, decreasing 2 (0, 5, 13, 9, 14, 17) sts evenly spaced around = 78 (80, 80, 82, 86, 86, 88) sts rem.

Change to smaller size circular and work 6 (6, 8, 8, 8, 8, 8) rnds in k1, p1 ribbing. BO in ribbing on last rnd.

### FINISHING

Weave in all ends neatly on WS. Seam underarms. Block pullover by covering it with a damp towel; leave until completely dry.

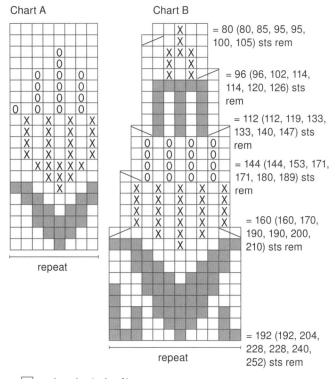

Chart A          Chart B

= 80 (80, 85, 95, 95, 100, 105) sts rem

= 96 (96, 102, 114, 114, 120, 126) sts rem

= 112 (112, 119, 133, 133, 140, 147) sts rem

= 144 (144, 153, 171, 171, 180, 189) sts rem

= 160 (160, 170, 190, 190, 200, 210) sts rem

= 192 (192, 204, 228, 228, 240, 252) sts rem

repeat          repeat

☐ main color (color A)

▨ color B

☒ color C

◻ color D

◸ sl 1, k1, psso with color A

◹ k2tog with color A

# Blanket for the Smallest Ones

Charming, simple cables for a delicate baby blanket. A doll size is included too, so the baby doll can have its own coverlet.

*Level 2*

**Sizes:** Doll blanket approx. 15¾ x 19¾ in (40 x 50 cm) [Baby blanket approx. 26½ x 30¾ in (67 x 78 cm)]

**MATERIALS**
**Yarn:** Sandnes Garn KlompeLompe Merinoull [CYCA #3 – DK, light worsted, 100% Merino wool, 114 yd (104 m) / 50 g]

**YARN COLORS AND AMOUNTS:**
Dark Gray-Blue 6061: 150 (350) g

**Needles:** U.S. size 7 (4.5 mm): 32 in (80 cm) circular; cable needle

**Gauge:** 20 sts = 4 in (10 cm).

Adjust needle size to obtain correct gauge if necessary.

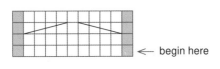

← begin here

| | slip 3 sts to cable needle and hold in back of work, k1, k3 from cable needle |

| | slip 1 st to cable needle and hold in front of work, k3, k1 from cable needle |

☐ knit on RS, purl on WS

■ purl on RS, knit on WS

CO 67 (133) sts.

Work 8 (20) rows in seed st (Row 1: *K1, p1*; rep * to * across. Subsequent rows: Work purl over knit and knit over purl.)

Place markers on last row of doll blanket: 19 seed sts, pm, 11 seed sts, pm, 7 seed sts, pm, 11 seed sts, pm, 19 seed sts.

Place markers on last row of baby blanket: 43 seed sts, pm, 11 seed sts, pm, 7 seed sts, pm, 11 seed sts, pm, 7 seed sts, pm, 11 seed sts, pm, 43 seed sts.

Now work the outermost 19 (43) sts at each side and each 7-st panel in seed st. The rem 2 (3) 11-st panels are worked following the cable chart.

Continue as est until blanket measures approx. 18½ (28¾) in [47 (73) cm] and you've just worked Row 1 of chart.

Finish with 8 (20) rows in seed st. BO in seed st.

**FINISHING**
Weave in all ends neatly on WS. Block blanket by covering it with a damp towel; leave until completely dry.

# Dinosaur Pullover

This pullover with dinosaurs around the yoke is knitted on small needles. That means it won't be too warm even if made in Merino wool.

*Level 2*

**Sizes:** 1 (2, 4, 6, 8, 10) years

**FINISHED MEASUREMENTS**
Chest: Approx. 21¾ (22, 24½, 27½, 29½, 30¼) in [55 (56, 62, 70, 75, 77) cm]

Total Length: Approx. 12¾ (14½, 15¾, 17½, 19, 20) in [32 (37, 40, 44.5, 48.5, 51) cm]

**MATERIALS**
**Yarn:** Sandnes Garn KlompeLompe Tynn Merinoull (fine Merino wool) [CYCA #1 – fingering, 100% Merino wool, 191 yd (175 m) / 50 g]

**YARN COLORS AND AMOUNTS:**
Color A: Blue-Petroleum 7251: 150 (150, 150, 200, 250, 250) g

Color B: Gray-Brown 2652: 50 (50, 50, 50, 50, 50) g

**Needles:** U.S. sizes 1.5 and 2.5 (2.5 and 3 mm): 16 and 24 in (40 and 60 cm) circulars and sets of 5 dpn

**Notions:** 2 (2, 2, 2, 2) buttons

**Gauge:** 27 sts on larger size needles = 4 in (10 cm).

Adjust needle size to obtain correct gauge if necessary.

The pullover is worked from the top down, beginning back and forth on a circular.

With color A and smaller size circular, CO 90 (94, 100, 100, 108, 108) sts. Work back and forth for 8 (8, 8, 10, 10, 10) rows (with buttonhole on row 4), with the first 5 and last 5 sts in garter st (knit all rows), and rem sts in k1, p1 ribbing.

**Note:** On the 5th row, make a buttonhole: Work as est until 4 sts rem, BO 2 sts, k2. On next row, CO 2 sts over gap.

Change to larger size circular. Knit 1 row, increasing 46 (50, 44, 52, 52, 52) sts evenly spaced between garter bands = 136 (144, 144, 152, 160, 160) sts.

Work 9 rows with stockinette between the garter st bands. On the 8th row, make a buttonhole as before. Knit 1 row, increasing 34 (36, 36, 38, 40, 40) sts evenly spaced between garter bands = 170 (180, 180, 190, 200, 200) sts.

Work 7 rows in stockinette and garter st as est. Knit 1 row, increasing 43 (49, 49, 38, 40, 40) sts evenly spaced between garter bands = 213 (229, 229, 228, 240, 240) sts.

Purl 1 row. On next row (RS), BO the first 5 sts and join to work in the round = 208 (224, 224, 223, 235, 235) sts rem.

Knit 0 (0, 2, 2, 4, 4) rnds.

Knit 0 (0, 1, 1, 1, 1) rnd increasing − (−, 0, 17, 21, 21) sts evenly spaced around = 208 (224, 224, 240, 256, 256) sts.

Now work around following chart.

After completing charted rows, you should have 234 (252, 252, 270, 288, 288) sts.

Knit 1 rnd. Knit next rnd, adjusting st count to 246 (258, 278, 304, 320, 332) sts.

With color A, knit 4 (4, 6, 6, 6, 8) rnds.

Place sleeve sts on holders as follows:

Place next 56 (60, 62, 64, 66, 69) sts on a holder (sleeve sts), CO 7 sts for underarm, k67 (69, 77, 88, 94, 97) for back, place next 56 (60, 62, 64, 66, 69) sts on a holder (sleeve sts), CO 7 sts for underarm, k67 (69, 77, 88, 94, 97) for front.

### FRONT AND BACK

There should now be 148 (152, 168, 190, 202, 208) sts for body. Work around in stockinette in color A until piece measures 11½ (13½, 14½, 16¼, 17¾, 18½) [29 (34, 37, 41, 45, 47) cm].

Change to smaller size circular and work in k1, p1 ribbing for 1¼ (1¼, 1¼, 1⅜, 1⅜, 1½) in [3 (3, 3, 3.5, 3.5, 4) cm]. BO in ribbing on last rnd.

### SLEEVES

With larger size dpn and color A, CO 4 sts, k56 (60, 62, 64, 66, 69) sts from holder, CO 3 sts.

Work sleeve in the round. The first st is a marked st and is purled throughout.

When sleeve is ¾ in (2 cm) long, begin shaping as follows: Knit until 2 sts before marked st, sl 1, k1, psso, p1 (marked st), k2tog.

Rep the decrease rnd every ⅝ (¾, ¾,1, 1, 1¼) in [1.5 (2, 2, 2.5, 2.5, 3) cm] until 45 (49, 49, 51, 52, 56) sts rem.

When sleeve is 7 (8¼, 9½, 10¾, 11¾, 13) in [18 (21, 24, 27, 30, 33) cm] long, knit 1 rnd, decreasing 1 (1, 1, 1, 1, 0) st.

Change to smaller size dpn and work around in k1, p1 ribbing for 1¼ (1¼, 1¼, 1⅜, 1⅜, 1½) in [3 (3, 3, 3.5, 3.5, 4) cm]. BO in ribbing on last rnd.

Knit second sleeve the same way.

### FINISHING

Seam underarms. Sew down short ends of back button band.

Weave in all ends neatly on WS.

Block pullover by covering it with a damp towel; leave until completely dry.

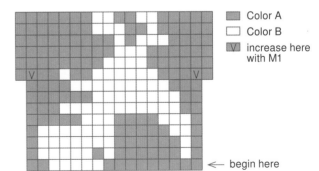

■ Color A
□ Color B
Ⅴ increase here with M1

← begin here

# Kurt Pants

Toasty striped pants for cold winter days. Perfect under a snowsuit or for relaxing in the stroller or baby carriage.

---

*Level 2*

- - - - - - - - - - - - - - - - - - - - - - - - - - - - - -

**Sizes:** 1 (2, 4, 6, 8, 10) years

**FINISHED MEASUREMENTS**
Waist: Approx. 19¾ (21, 22½, 23¾, 25¼, 27¼) in [50 (53, 57, 60, 64, 69) cm]

Length: Approx. 14¼ (17¼, 22¾, 26¾, 29¾, 33) in [36 (44, 58, 68, 75, 84) cm]

**MATERIALS**
Yarn: Sandnes Garn KlompeLompe Spøt [CYCA #3 – DK, light worsted, 40% Merino wool, 40% alpaca, 20% nylon, 147 yd (134 m) / 50 g]

**YARN COLORS AND AMOUNTS:**
Color A: Light Gray-Brown 2370: 100 (100, 100, 150, 150, 200) g

Color B: Blue Petroleum 7251: 50 (100 100, 100, 100, 150) g

**Needles:** U.S. sizes 2.5 and 4 (3 and 3.5 mm): 24 and 32 in (60 and 80 cm) circulars and sets of 5 dpn

**Notions:** Waistband elastic long enough to go around waist + seam allowance

**Gauge:** 22 sts in stockinette on larger size needles = 4 in (10 cm).

Adjust needle size to obtain correct gauge if necessary.

- - - - - - - - - - - - - - - - - - - - - - - - - - - - - -

The pants are worked top down, in the round on circular needles.

With color A and smaller size circular, CO 112 (120, 128, 136, 144, 156) sts. Join, being careful not to twist cast-on row; pm for beginning of rnd.

Knit 15 rnds. Purl 1 rnd (foldline). Work 15 rnds k2, p2 ribbing.

Change to larger size circular. Knit 1 rnd.

Lengthen back of pants with short rows as follows:

K10; turn, yo. P20; turn, yo. Knit until 4 sts past last turn (when you come to it, knit yarnover together with following st); turn, yo. Purl until 4 sts past last turn. Continue as est until you've turned a total of 4 (5, 5, 6, 6, 7) times on each side.

Continue in stockinette. When you come to yarnover when you last turned, knit st before yarnover together with yarnover. Knit to beginning of rnd.

**STRIPES**
*Change to color B. Knit 2 rnds.

Change to color A. Knit 2 rnds.*

Rep * to *.

Continue in stripe pattern until piece measures 4 (4¾, 5½, 6¼, 7, 7½) in [10 (12, 14, 16, 18, 19) cm] from rnd where you changed to larger size needle. Place 2 markers at center front and two markers at center back with 10 sts between each pair of markers.

Inc 1 st with M1 on each side of the 10 marked sts at back and front. Increase the same way on every 3rd rnd 5 times = 132 (140, 148, 156, 164, 176) sts. BO the center 10 marked sts on back and front on next rnd = 56 (60, 64, 68, 72, 78) sts rem for each leg.

Work each leg separately, in the round.

The first st on the rnd is always purled = marked st. Continue in stripe pattern.

Knit as est for 1¼ in (3 cm). Begin shaping leg: Decrease with k2tog to eliminate 1 st before and 1 st after marked st. Decrease the same way every ¾ (¾, 1¼, 1¼, 1¼, 1¼) in 2 (2, 3, 3, 3, 3) cm] a total of 5 (5, 6, 6, 7, 7) times.

Continue in stockinette and stripes until pants measure 11½ (14½, 20, 24, 26¾, 30¼) in [29 (37, 51, 61, 68, 77) cm] from rnd where you changed to larger size needle.

**Next Rnd:** Decrease 6 (6, 8, 8, 6, 8) sts evenly spaced around = 40 (44, 44, 48, 52, 56) sts rem.

Change to smaller size dpn. With color A, work around in k2, p2 ribbing for 2¾ in (7 cm). BO in ribbing.

Knit the other leg the same way.

**FINISHING**
Join the crotch sets of 10 sts on back and front with Kitchener st.

Seam short ends of waistband elastic. Fold in waist at foldline. Insert elastic and sew down casing.

Weave in all ends neatly on WS.

Block pants by covering with a damp towel; leave until completely dry.

# Rambaskår Sweater-Jacket

Many are the times we've taken a hike up Rambaskår with a little one in a carrier or with hands tightly gripped as we forged ahead. We're always happy to hike in the local area, and, for that reason, we named this jacket after one of our destinations. We designed two versions of this jacket, each with a different texture pattern. One version is a bit easier and quicker to knit than the other, which has a charming and somewhat more time-consuming lace pattern.

*Level 3*

**Sizes:** 0–1 (3, 6–12, 18–24) months

**FINISHED MEASUREMENTS**

Chest: Approx. 16½ (19, 21¼, 23¾) in [42 (48, 54, 60) cm]

Total Length: Approx. 9 (11¼, 13, 15¾) in [23 (28.5, 33, 40) cm]

**MATERIALS**

**Yarn:** Sandnes Garn KlompeLompe Tynn Merinoull (fine Merino wool) [CYCA #1 – fingering, 100% Merino wool, 191 yd (175 m) / 50 g]

**YARN COLORS AND AMOUNTS:**

Gray-Brown 2652: 100 (100, 150, 200) g

**Needles:** U.S. sizes 1.5 and 2.5 (2.5 and 3 mm): 24 in (60 cm) circulars and sets of 5 dpn

**Notions:** 8 (8, 8, 9) buttons

**Gauge:** 27 sts on larger size needles = 4 in (10 cm).

Adjust needle size to obtain correct gauge if necessary.

The sweater is worked bottom up, back and forth on a circular.

**WAVE PATTERN VERSION**

With smaller size circular, CO 116 (136, 152, 166) sts. Work back and forth in k1, p1 ribbing with garter st bands, set up as follows: K5 (edge sts), pm, work 46 (56, 66, 71) sts in k1, p1 ribbing (pattern sts), pm, work 60 (70, 76, 85) sts in k1, p1 ribbing, pm, k5 (edge sts).

The outermost 5 sts at each side are always knitted (garter st) while rem sts are worked in k1, p1 ribbing. Continue as est and, on row 5, make a buttonhole: k2, k2tog, yo, k1, rib until 5 sts rem, k5.

After completing a total of 8 rows, change to larger size circular. Continuing with 5 garter sts at each side, work in pattern following chart on the 46 (56, 66, 71) sts pattern sts previously in k1, p1 ribbing. Work rem sts in stockinette.

Make a buttonhole every 1¼ (1½, 1½, 2) in [3 (4, 4, 5) cm] = a total of 8 (8, 8, 9) buttonholes.

When piece measures approx. 5½ (7, 8¼, 10¼) in [14 (18, 21, 26) cm] and next row is on RS, shape underarms as follows: K5, work in pattern to next marker, BO 4 sts, knit until 4 sts before marker, BO 4 sts, k5. Set piece aside.

## BLOCK PATTERN VERSION

With smaller size circular, CO 121 (145, 157, 171) sts. Work back and forth in k1, p1 ribbing with garter st bands, set up as follows: K5 (edge sts), pm, work 49 (61, 67, 73) sts in k1, p1 ribbing (pattern sts), pm, work 62 (74, 80, 88) sts in k1, p1 ribbing, pm, k5 (edge sts).

The outermost 5 sts at each side are always knitted (garter st) while rem sts are worked in k1 p1 ribbing. Continue as est and, on row 5, make a buttonhole: k2, k2tog, yo, k1, rib until 5 sts rem, k5.

After completing a total of 8 rows, change to larger size circular. Continuing with 5 garter sts at each side, work in pattern following chart on the 49 (61, 67, 73) sts pattern sts previously in k1, p1 ribbing. Work rem sts in stockinette.

Make a buttonhole every 1¼ (1⅜, 1½, 2) in [3 (3.5, 4, 5) cm = a total of 8 (8, 8, 9) buttonholes.

When piece measures approx. 5½ (7, 8¼, 10¼) in [14 (18, 21, 26) cm] and next row is on RS, shape underarms as follows: K5, work in pattern to next marker, BO 4 sts, knit until 4 sts before marker, BO 4 sts, k5. Set piece aside.

## SLEEVES

With smaller size dpn, CO 40 (40, 42, 42) sts. Divide sts onto dpn and join. Work around in k1, p1 ribbing for 8 rnds. Change to larger size dpn.

Work in stockinette, but, always purl the first st as a marked st.

After ⅜ in (1 cm) in stockinette, begin shaping sleeve as follows:

P1, M1, knit to end of rnd M1.

Increase the same way approx. every 1¼ (¾, ⅝, ¾) in [3 (2, 1.5, 2) cm] until there are 46 (52, 60, 62) sts. Continue in stockinette until sleeve is 5½ (6¼, 8, 9¾) in [14 (16, 20, 25) cm] long. BO 4 sts centered on underarm. Set first sleeve aside while you knit second sleeve the same way.

Arrange sleeves on same circular as body, matching underarms.

The first row is on WS. Pm at each intersection of body and sleeve = 4 markers.

Don't forget to work the 5 outermost sts at each side in garter st and work in pattern on the front.

On every RS row:

K4, sl 1, k1, psso, work in pattern until 2 sts before marker, *sl 1, k1, psso, k2tog, knit until 2 sts before next marker*; rep * to * 2 more times, k1, k2tog, k4.

**Note:** The last st of the 5 garter sts (buttonband) is decreased into body but continues up as a garter st.

Decrease as above on every RS row. After 15 (18, 22, 25) decrease rows, and next row is on RS, change to smaller size circular. Work 6 rows in k1, p1 ribbing inside the outermost 5 sts at each side. On the 3rd row make the last buttonhole. BO in ribbing on last row.

## FINISHING

Seam underarms and sew on buttons.

Weave in all ends neatly on WS.

Block sweater by gently steam pressing under a damp pressing cloth or by covering it with a damp towel; leave until completely dry.

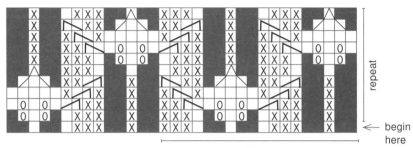

repeat

← begin here

repeat

■ no stitch

☐ knit on RS, purl on WS

☒ purl on RS, knit on WS

◻0◻ yarnover

◿ k2tog on RS p2tog on WS

◺ sl 1, k1, psso (or ssk: *sl 2 knitwise, one at a time, return sts to left needle and k2tog tbl (or p2tog* on WS)

◮ sl 1, k2tog, psso (*sl 1, p2tog, psso* on WS)

knit 2nd st on left needle in front of 1st st, do not drop st off needle, purl 1st st; slip both sts off left needle (same on WS)

purl 2nd st on left needle behind 1st st, do not drop st off needle, knit 1st st; slip both sts off left needle (same on WS)

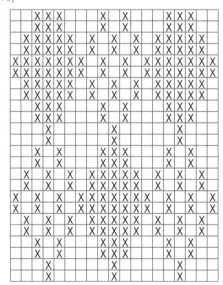

☐ knit on RS, purl on WS

☒ purl on RS, knit on WS

← begin here

# Rambaskår Pants

Knit an easy pair of pants to go with the Rambaskår sweater-jacket. The pants feature the same texture pattern down the sides as for the sweater. The two garments make a perfect set for small children.

*Level 2*

**Sizes:** 0–1 (1–3, 6, 12, 18–24) months

**FINISHED MEASUREMENTS**
Waist: Approx. 16½ (17¾, 19, 19½, 20) in [42 (45, 48, 49.5, 51) cm]

Leg Length: Approx. 4¾ (6¼, 7½, 8¾, 9¾) in [12 (16, 19, 22, 25) cm]

**MATERIALS**
**Yarn:** Sandnes Garn KlompeLompe Tynn Merinoull (fine Merino wool) [CYCA #1 – fingering, 100% Merino wool, 191 yd (175 m) / 50 g]

**YARN COLORS AND AMOUNTS:**
Powder Pink 4344: 100 (100, 100, 150, 150) g

**Needles:** U.S. sizes 1.5 and 2.5 (2.5 and 3 mm): 16 in (40 cm) circulars and sets of 5 dpn

**Notions:** Waistband elastic long enough to go around waist + seam allowance; 2 buttons

**Gauge:** 27 sts in stockinette on larger size needles = 4 in (10 cm).

Adjust needle size to obtain correct gauge if necessary.

The pants are worked top down, in the round.

With smaller size circular, CO 114 (122, 130, 134, 138) sts. Join, being careful not to twist cast-on row; pm for beginning of rnd.

Work 20 rnds k1, p1 ribbing.

Change to larger size circular. Knit 1 rnd, increasing 12 (12 12, 16, 16) sts evenly spaced around = 126 (134, 142, 150, 154) sts.

Lengthen back of pants with short rows. When turning, wrap yarn around next st before you turn, and knit the wrap with its st when you later come to it.

K10; turn. P20; turn. K25; turn. P30; turn. K35; turn. P40; (on size 0–1 month, work back to beginning of rnd and omit the last 2 turns); turn. K45; turn, p50; turn. Knit to beginning of rnd (= k25).

Pm for pattern panel:

K27 (29, 31, 33, 34), pm, 9 sts pattern, pm, k54 (58, 62, 66, 68), pm, 9 sts pattern, pm, kK27 (29, 31, 33, 34).

When pants measure 5¼ (5, 6¾, 7½, 8¾) in [13 (15, 17, 19, 22) cm] down front, pm on each side of the center 6 sts at front and back. Increase on each side of the 6 sts with M1.

Increase the same way every 1¼ in (3 cm) a total of 5 (6, 6, 6, 6) times = 20 (24, 24, 24, 24) sts increased = 146 (158, 166, 174, 178) sts. On next rnd, BO 6 center sts on front and back. Work each leg separately, in the round = 67 (73, 77, 81, 83) sts rem for each leg.

Join the two 6-st sets of crotch on back and front with Kitchener st (see page 7). Sew a button on each leg.

Seam short ends of waistband elastic. Insert elastic. Fold waist ribbing in half and sew down casing.

Weave in all ends neatly on WS.

Block pants by covering with a damp towel; leave until completely dry.

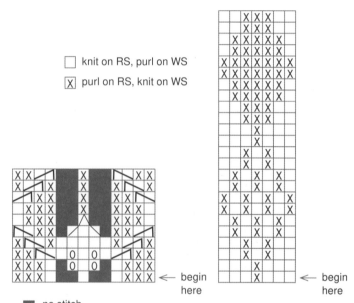

☐ knit on RS, purl on WS

☒ purl on RS, knit on WS

← begin here

← begin here

■ no stitch

☐ knit

☒ purl

◻ yarnover

◪ k2tog

◪ sl 1, k1, psso

◪ sl 1, k2tog, psso

◪ knit 2nd st on left needle in front of 1st st, do not drop st off needle, purl 1st st; slip both sts off left needle

◪ purl 2nd st on left needle behind 1st st, do not drop st off needle, knit 1st st; slip both sts off left needle

Divide sts of one leg onto larger size dpn and work in the round in stockinette and with pattern down outside of leg. When leg measures ⅜ (⅜, ¾, 1¼, 1½) in [1 (1, 2, 3, 4) cm], decrease as follows:

K1, k2tog, work until 3 sts rem, sl 1, k1, psso, k1.

Decrease the same way every ¾ in (2 cm) a total of 4 (6, 7, 8, 8) times and then work without decreasing until leg measures approx. 4 (5½, 6¾, 8, 9) in [10 (14, 17, 20, 23) cm] = 59 (61, 63, 65, 67) sts rem. The side pattern is now finished.

Knit 1 rnd, adjusting stitch count to 48 (50, 50, 52, 52) sts.

Change to smaller size dpn and work 24 rnds in k1 p1 ribbing, **but**, *after 18 rnds*, make a buttonhole at the side as follows: Rib 23 (24, 24, 25, 25), BO 2 sts, rib 23 (24, 24, 25, 25) sts. On next rnd CO 2 sts over gap. BO in ribbing on Rnd 24. Make second leg the same way.

# Flutter-About Scarf

A decorative pull-through scarf that stays in place well.
Perfect for the littlest ones.

*Level 2*

---

**Sizes:** 1–6 (6–12 months, 1–3, 4–6 years)

**MATERIALS**
**Yarn:** Sandnes Garn KlompeLompe Merinoull [CYCA #3 – DK, light worsted, 100% Merino wool, 114 yd (104 m) / 50 g]

**YARN COLORS AND AMOUNTS:**
Powder Rose 4032: 50 (50, 50, 100) g

**Needles:** U.S. size 4 (3.5 mm): set of 5 dpn

**Gauge:** 22 sts= 4 in (10 cm).

Adjust needle size to obtain correct gauge if necessary.

---

CO 21 (23, 25, 27) sts.

Work 6 rows in seed st:

**SEED STITCH**
**Row 1:** *K1, p1*; rep * to * across.

**Subsequent Rows:** Work Purl over knit and knit over purl.

Now work 6 (7, 8, 9) seed sts, 9 sts charted pattern, 6 (7, 8, 9) seed sts.

Continue as est with seed st at each side and pattern in center until you've repeated pattern 2 (2, 2, 3) times. Divide sts with every other st on a new needle. Work each side separately with 10 rows k1, p1 ribbing.

Now re-join all sts: alternately place 1 st from front needle and then 1 st from back needle onto same needle.

Continue in seed st and pattern until you've worked 8 (9, 10, 12) repeats.

Work 10 rows in k1, p1 ribbing.

Continue in seed st and pattern until you've worked 2 (2, 2, 3) repeats.

Finish with 6 rows seed st and BO in seed st on last row.

**FINISHING**
Weave in all ends neatly on WS.

Block scarf by covering it with a damp towel; leave until completely dry.

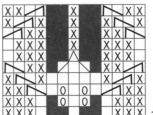

← begin here

■ no stitch

☐ knit on RS, purl on WS

☒ purl on RS, knit on WS

⓪ yarnover

╱ k2tog (p2tog on WS)

⧄ sl 1, k2tog, psso (*sl 1, p2tog, psso* on WS)

╲ sl 1, k1, psso (*sl 1, p2tog, psso* on WS)

◹ knit 2nd st on left needle in front of 1st st, do not drop st off needle, purl 1st st; slip both sts off left needle (same on WS)

◺ purl 2nd st on left needle behind 1st st, do not drop st off needle, knit 1st st; slip both sts off left needle (same on WS)

# Olle Ball Cap

Soft and thick, this cap is knitted on big needles with two strands of yarn held together. A pretty knot structure and a little knot at the top make this a project you'll want to knit more of.

## Level 1

**Sizes:** 3–5 (6–12 months, 1–3, 3–6) years

**MATERIALS**
**Yarn:** Sandnes Garn KlompeLompe Spøt [CYCA #3 – DK, light worsted, 40% Merino wool, 40% alpaca, 20% nylon, 147 yd (134 m) / 50 g]

**YARN COLORS AND AMOUNTS:**
Flax Blue 6051: 100 (100, 100, 100) g

**Needles:** U.S. size 8 (5 mm): 16 in (40 cm) circular and U.S. sizes 6 and 8 (4 and 5 mm): sets of 5 dpn

**Gauge:** 17 sts with yarn held double on larger size needles = 4 in (10 cm).

Adjust needle size to obtain correct gauge if necessary.

The cap begins with the cord tie on the earflaps.

With smaller size dpn and single strand of yarn, CO 4 sts. Knit an I-cord 7 in (18 cm) long (see page 7 and video at kompelompe.no).

**EARFLAP**
With two strands of yarn held together and larger size dpn, work first row on WS as follows:

**Row 1:** P1, k1, M1, k1, p1.

**Row 2 (RS):** In first st, p1 in front loop and k1 in back loop, p1, k1, p1, k1 in front loop and p1 in back loop of last st.

**Row 3:** *K1, p1*; rep * to * across.

**Row 4 (RS):** In first st, k1 in front loop and p1 in back loop, k1, p1, k1 p1 k1, p1 in front loop and k1 in back loop of last st.

**Row 5:** *P1, k1*; rep * to * across.

Continue increasing and ribbing as est until there are 15 (17, 17, 19) sts. Work last row on WS. Set earflap aside while you make second one the same way.

CO 3 sts, work in ribbing across one earflap, CO 19 (21, 25, 25) sts, rib across second earflap, CO 2 sts = 54 (60, 65, 68) sts. Join and pm at beginning of rnd. Work in k1, p1 ribbing for 7 (8, 8, 9) rnds.

Knit 1 rnd, increasing 6 (6, 8, 4) sts evenly spaced around = 60 (66, 72, 72) sts.

**KNOT PATTERN**
P3tog but do not drop sts off left needle, k3tog (same sts), p3tog. Now slip sts off left needle.

Begin Knot Pattern on Cap:

**Rnds 1–3:** Knit.

**Rnd 4:** *K3, knot*; rep * to * around.

**Rnds 5–7:** Knit.

**Rnd 8:** *Knot, k3*; rep * to * around.

**Note:** On sizes 3–5 months and 1–3 years, begin with knit 3 rnds and then work Rnd 4 as: *Knot, k3*; rep * to * around.

After working 4 (5, 6, 7) rnds of knots, continue as follows (change to dpn when sts no longer fit around circular):

**Rnds 1–2.** Knit.

**Rnd 3:** *K4, k2tog*; rep * to * around.

**Rnd 4:** *Knot, k2*; rep * to * around.

**Rnds 5–6:** Knit.

**Rnd 7:** *K2tog, k3*; rep * to * around.

**Rnds 8–9:** Knit.

**Rnd 10:** *K2, k2tog*; rep * to * around.

**Rnds 11–12:** Knit.

**Rnd 13:** *K1, k2tog*; rep * to * around.

**Rnd 14:** Knit.

**Rnd 15:** *K2tog*; rep * to * around.

**Rnd 16:** *K1, k2tog*; rep * to * around until 4 (2, 0, 0) sts rem, k4 (2, 0, 0) = 8 sts rem.

Knit rem 8 sts around for 4 in (10 cm). Cut yarn and draw end through rem sts; tighten.

**FINISHING**
Weave in all ends neatly on WS.

Block cap by covering it with a damp towel; leave until completely dry.

# Wing Union Suit

Our favorite union suit for girls. Cozy, thick, and warm around the body, while fine and loose around the arms. The wings are the icing on the cake and make the outfit more special than just another outfit for nursery school. (Even though it's also great for wearing to nursery school!)

*Level 3*

- - - - - - - - - - - - - - - - - - - - - - - - - - -

**Sizes:** 0–1 (3, 6–9 months, 1, 2, 4 years)

**FINISHED MEASUREMENTS**
Chest: Approx. 18¾ (18¾, 20, 21, 22½, 23¾) in [47.5 (47.5, 51, 53, 57.5, 60) cm]

Total Length: Approx. 18½ (21¾, 23¾, 24¼, 30, 32¼) in [47 (55, 60, 69, 76, 82) cm]

**MATERIALS**
**Yarn:** Sandnes Garn KlompeLompe Merinoull [CYCA #3 – DK, light worsted, 100% Merino wool, 114 yd (104 m) / 50 g]

Sandnes Garn KlompeLompe Tynn Merinoull (fine Merino wool) [CYCA #1 – fingering, 100% Merino wool, 191 yd (175 m) / 50 g]

**YARN COLORS AND AMOUNTS:**
Merinoull Blue-Petroleum 7251: 100 (150, 150, 200, 250, 250) g

Tynn Merinoull Blue-Petroleum 7251: 100 (100, 100, 100, 150, 150) g

**Needles:** U.S. sizes 1.5, 2.5, and 4 (2.5, 3, and 3.5 mm): 16 and 32 in (40 and 80 cm) circulars and sets of 5 dpn

**Notions:** 6 (6, 7, 7, 8, 8) buttons

**Gauge:** 22 sts on needles U.S. 4 (3.5 mm) and 27 sts on needles U.S. 2.5 (3 mm) = 4 in (10 cm).

Adjust needle size to obtain correct gauge if necessary.

- - - - - - - - - - - - - - - - - - - - - - - - - - -

The garment is worked bottom up.

With Merinoull and U.S. 2.5 (3 mm) dpn, CO 34 (34, 38, 42, 46, 46) sts. Divide sts onto dpn and join. Work 16 rnds k1, p1 ribbing.

Change to dpn U.S. 4 (3.5 mm) and knit 1 rnd.

Knit next rnd, increasing (with M1) 10 sts evenly spaced around.

Knit around in stockinette for 4¼ (5¼, 6¼, 8, 9, 9¾) in [11 (13, 16, 20, 23, 25) cm], *but*, after ¾ (¾, 1¼, 2, 2, 2) in [2 (2, 3, 5, 5, 5) cm], increase as follows: K1, M1, knit until 1 st rem, M1, k1. Increase the same way every ¾ (1, 1¼, 1½, 1½, 1⅜) in [2 (2.5, 3, 4, 4, 3.5) cm] a total of 5 (5, 5, 4, 5, 6) times = 54 (54, 58, 60, 66, 68) sts. Set piece aside and make a second leg the same way.

116, 128, 132) sts rem. Begin working back and forth at this point.

Work back and forth in stockinette until body is 8 (9¾, 11,12¼, 13¾, 15½) in [20 (25, 28, 31, 35, 39) cm] above crotch.

Lengthen back with short rows as follows: (there is a yarn-over after each turn; when you later come to one, knit/purl the yarnover with next st).

Knit to marker at center back, k20; turn, yo. P40; turn, yo. K35; turn, yo. P30; turn, yo. K25; turn, yo. P20; turn, yo; knit to end of row.

Purl 1 row.

Change to Tynn Merinoull and U.S. 2.5 (3 mm) circular. Knit 1 row, increasing 24 (24, 26, 28, 28, 30) sts evenly spaced across = 128 (128, 138, 144, 156, 162) sts. Knit 1 row on WS. Work in stockinette for ¾ in (2 cm).

Now divide body for front and back: K23 (23, 24, 25, 28, 29), BO 16 (16, 19, 20, 20, 21) sts, k50 (50, 52, 54, 60, 62), BO 16 (16, 19, 20, 20, 21) sts, k23 (23, 24, 25, 28, 29).

**LEFT FRONT**
The first row is WS.

Purl 1 row.

**Next Row:** K1, k2tog, knit to end of row.

Rep these two rows a total of 4 times = 19 (19, 20, 21, 24, 25) sts rem.

Continue back and forth in stockinette until front measures 2¾ (2¾, 3½, 3½, 4, 4) in [7 (7, 9, 9, 10, 10) cm] above purl rnd. On next row (WS), with extra needle, purl the first 8 (8, 8, 8, 10, 10) sts. Purl rem 11 (11, 12, 13, 14, 15) sts for shoulder.

**Next Row:** Knit until 3 sts rem, k2 tog, k1.

Purl next row.

Rep these two rows a total of 4 times.

Work in stockinette for ¾ (¾, 1¼, 1¼, 1¼,1¼) in [2 (2, 3, 3, 3, 3) cm].

On next, RS, row, BO knitwise.

With Merinoull and U.S. 4 (3.5 mm) circular, CO 4 sts. Knit leg 1, CO 8 sts, knit leg 2, CO 4 sts = 124 (124, 132, 136, 148, 152) sts total. The rnd begins here at center front.

Pm at center front and pm centered on back, around the 8 sts cast on. Knit 1 rnd, decreasing on every other rnd: *K4, sl 1 k1, psso, knit until 6 sts before next marker, k2tog, k4*; rep * to * = 4 sts decreased around.

Repeat the decrease rnd (on every other rnd) a total of 4 times = 108 (108, 116, 120, 132, 136) sts rem.

Continue around in stockinette until body measures 2½ (2¾, 4, 4¾, 4¾, 4¾) in [6 (7, 10, 12, 12, 12) cm] above crotch. BO 2 sts before and 2 sts after first marker = 104 (104, 112,

## RIGHT FRONT

The first row is WS.

Purl 1 row.

**Next Row:** Knit until 3 sts rem, sl 1, k1, psso, k1.

Rep these two rows a total of 4 times = 19 (19, 20, 21, 24, 25) sts rem.

Continue back and forth in stockinette until front measures 2¾ (2¾, 3½, 3½, 4, 4) in [7 (7, 9, 9. 10, 10) cm] above purl rnd. On next row (WS), with extra needle, purl the last 8 (8, 8, 8, 10, 10) sts.

Cut yarn and work the rem 11 (11, 12, 13, 14, 15) sts for shoulder.

**Next Row:** K1, k2tog, knit to end of row.

Purl next row.

Rep these two rows a total of 4 times.

Work in stockinette for ¾ (¾, 1¼, 1¼, 1¼,1¼) in [2 (2, 3, 3, 3, 3) cm].

On next, RS, row, BO knitwise.

## BACK

The first row is WS.

Purl 1 row.

**Next Row:** K1, k2tog, knit until 3 sts rem, sl 1, k1, psso, k1.

Rep these two rows a total of 4 times.

Continue back and forth in stockinette without decreasing until piece measures 3½ (3½, 4¼, 4¼, 4¾, 4¾) in 9 (9, 11, 11, 12, 12) cm] above purl round.

The next row is on WS: purl the first 31 (31, 32, 33, 38, 39) onto an extra needle and purl the last 11 (11, 12, 13, 14, 15) sts for left strap.

**Next Row:** Knit until 3 sts rem, k2tog, k1.

Purl across next row.

Rep these two rows a total of 4 times.

On next, RS, row, BO knitwise.

**RS:** Knit the first 11 (11, 12, 13, 14, 15) sts onto an extra needle for right strap.

**Next Row:** K1, k2tog, knit to end of row.

Purl next row.

Rep these two rows a total of 4 times.

On next, RS, row, BO knitwise.

Seam shoulders.

### FRONT BANDS

With Tynn Merinoull and U.S. 1.5 (2.5 mm) circular, pick up and knit sts on right front for buttonhole band. Pick up and knit 1 st in every st until you get to section with Tynn Merinoull in which you will pick up 3 sts and skip every 4th st. Work 8 rows k1, p1 ribbing, **but**, *on the 3rd row*, make 5 (5, 6, 6, 7, 7) buttonholes evenly spaced apart. For each buttonhole, BO 2 sts and CO 2 sts over each gap on 4th row.

BO in ribbing on last row.

**Note:** The 6th (6th, 7th, 7th, 8th, 8th) buttonhole will be made on the neckband.

Make the button band on left front as for buttonhole band, omitting buttonholes.

### RIBBED NECKBAND

With Tynn Merinoull and U.S. 1.5 (2.5 mm) circular, pick up and knit 6 sts along end of button band, k8 (8, 8, 8, 10, 10) sts from holder, pick up and knit 18 (18, 22, 22, 22, 22) sts on shoulder, k20 (20, 20 20, 24, 24) sts from holder, pick up and knit 18 (18, 22, 22, 22, 22) sts on shoulder, k8 (8, 8, 8, 10, 10) sts from holder, pick up and knit 6 sts along end of button band = 84 (84, 92, 92, 100, 100) sts total.

Work 8 rows k1, p1 ribbing, **but**, *on the 3rd row*, make a buttonhole: rib until 5 sts rem, BO 2 sts, rib 3. On next row, CO 2 sts over gap. Complete ribbing rows and BO in ribbing on last row.

### SLEEVES

With Tynn Merinoull and U.S. 2.5 (3 mm) needles. Beginning at center of underarm, pick up and knit 79 (79, 85, 85, 89, 89) sts around armhole. Join and knit 1 rnd.

Now change to working back and forth to shape sleeve cap with short rows.

**Note:** There is a yarnover after each turn; when you later come to one, knit/purl the yarnover with next st).

**Sizes 0–1 and 3 months:** K61; turn, yo. P45; turn, yo. K46; turn, yo. P47; turn, yo. K48; turn, yo. P49; turn, yo. K50; turn, yo. P51; turn, yo. K52, k2tog; turn, yo. P54, p2tog; turn, yo. K56, k2tog; turn, yo. P58, p2tog; turn, yo. K60, k2tog; turn, yo. P62, p2tog; turn, yo. K64, k2tog; turn, yo. P66, p2tog; turn. K69. You are now back at beginning of row = 71 sts. Knit to end of row.

**Sizes 6–9 months and 1 year:** K67; turn, yo. P51; turn, yo. K52; turn, yo. P53; turn, yo. K54; turn, yo. P55; turn, yo. K56; turn, yo. P57; turn, yo. K58, k2tog; turn, yo. P60, p2tog; turn, yo. K62, k2tog; turn, yo. P64, p2tog; turn, yo. K66, k2tog; turn, yo. P68, p2tog; turn, yo. K70, k2tog; turn, yo. P72, p2tog; turn. K75. You are now back at beginning of row = 77 sts. Knit to end of row.

**Sizes 2 and 4 years:** K71; turn, yo. P55; turn, yo. K56; turn, yo. P57; turn, yo. K58; turn, yo. P59; turn, yo. K60; turn, yo. P61; turn, yo. K62 k2tog; turn, yo. P64, p2tog; turn, yo. K66, k2tog; turn, yo. P68, p2tog; turn, yo. K70, k2tog; turn, yo. P72, p2tog; turn, yo. K74, k2tog; turn, yo. P76, p2tog; turn. K79. You are now back at beginning of row = 81 sts. Knit to end of row.

**ALL SIZES:**

Return to working in the round. Knit 1 rnd. Knit next rnd, decreasing 8 sts evenly spaced around. Knit 3 rnds. Knit 1 rnd, decreasing 8 sts evenly spaced around = 55 (55, 61, 61, 65, 65) sts rem.

Continue in stockinette until sleeve measures 4¾ (5½, 6¾, 7½, 9½, 10¾) in [12 (14, 17, 19, 24, 27) cm], *but, after ⅝ in (1.5 cm),* decrease as follows: K1, k2tog, knit until 3 sts rem, sl 1, k1, psso k1. Decrease the same way every ⅝ (¾, ¾, ¾, 1, 1¼) in [1.5 (2, 2, 2, 2.5, 3) cm] until 41 (43, 45, 45, 49, 49) sts rem. Knit 1 rnd, decreasing 1 st.

Change to U.S. 1.5 (2.5 mm) dpn and work around in k1, p1 ribbing for 1⅜ in (3.5 cm). BO in ribbing on last rnd.

Make the second sleeve the same way.

## WINGS

**Note:** After turning, slip first st and tighten yarn slightly.

With U.S. 2.5 (3 mm) circular, pick up and knit sts in a straight line from lower edge of stockinette section on front to lower edge of stockinette section on back.

For left wing, begin picking up sts on front and, for right wing, begin picking up sts on back. Pick up and knit sts in the last row before the shoulders. Pick up 1 st in each st on yoke.

Knit 2 rows.

K16 (16, 18, 18, 20, 20), increase with M1 after every 6th st until 16 (16, 18, 18, 20, 20) sts rem; turn.

Knit until 16 (16, 18, 18, 20, 20) sts rem; turn.

Knit until 5 sts before previous turn; turn.

Knit until 5 sts before previous turn; turn.

Knit, increasing with M1 after every 7th st until 5 sts before previous turn; turn.

Knit to end of row.

Knit 1 row.

BO knitwise.

Sew down tips of wings to body.

## FINISHING

Weave in all ends neatly on WS.

Sew on buttons.

Block garment by covering it with a damp towel; leave until completely dry.

# Albertine Cap

The pattern on this cap can be bit challenging to begin with. Once you learn the technique, though, it moves right along. Knitted with two colors, it's unbelievably appealing.

*Level 2*

**Sizes:** 6–9 months (1–2, 3–6, 7–10 years)

**MATERIALS**

**Yarn:** Sandnes Garn KlompeLompe Merinoull [CYCA #3 – DK, light worsted, 100% Merino wool, 114 yd (104 m) / 50 g]

**YARN COLORS AND AMOUNTS:**

Color A: Gray-Brown 2652: 50 (50, 50, 50) g

Color B: Powder Rose 4032: 50 (50, 50, 50) g

**Needles:** U.S. sizes 2.5 and 4 (3 and 3.5 mm): 16 in (40 cm) circulars and sets of 5 dpn or 32 in (80 cm) circular for magic loop; optional cable needle

**Notions:** optional—faux fur pom-pom

**Gauge:** 22 sts on larger size needles = 4 in (10 cm).

Adjust needle size to obtain correct gauge if necessary.

**STITCHES AND TECHNIQUES**

**RIGHT TWIST (RT)**

*Option 1:* Skip 1st st but leave it on left needle. Knit 2nd st with color A in front of 1st st. Knit 1st st with color B.

*Option 2:* Place 1st st on cable needle and hold in back of work. Knit 2nd st (in front of st on cable needle) with color A. K1 from cable needle with color B.

**LEFT TWIST (LT)**

*Option 1:* Skip 1st st but leave it on left needle. Knit 2nd st with color B in back of 1st st. Knit 1st st with color A.

*Option 2:* Place 1st st on cable needle and hold in front of work. Knit 2nd st (behind st on cable needle) with color B. K1 from cable needle with color A.

With color A and smaller size circular, CO 76 (80, 84, 90) sts. Join, being careful not to twist cast-on row; pm for beginning of rnd. Work 10 rnds in k1, p1 ribbing.

Change to larger size circular. Knit 1 rnd, increasing 14 (16, 18, 18) sts evenly spaced around = 90 (96, 102, 108) sts.

Now begin working in pattern:

**Rnd 1:** *K2 with color B, k2 with color A, k2 with color B*; rep * to * around.

**Rnd 2:** With color B only, *K2, sl 2, k2*; rep * to * around.

**Rnd 3:** Work as for Rnd 1.

**Rnd 4:** Work as for Rnd 2.

**Rnd 5:** *K1 with color B, RT, LT, k1 with color B*; rep * to * around.

**Rnd 6:** With color B only, *K1, sl 1, k2, sl 1, k1*; rep * to * around.

**Knitting Tips:** Make sure you don't knit too tightly and that the color A floats on the back; do not pull in.

**Rnd 7:** *RT, k2 with color B, LT*; rep * to * around.

**Rnd 8:** With color B only, *Sl 1, k4, sl 1*; rep * to * around.

**Rnd 9:** K1 with color A, k4 with color B, k1 with color A*; rep * to * around.

**Rnd 10:** With color B only, *Sl 1, k4, sl 1*; rep * to * around.

**Rnd 11:** Work as for Rnd 9.

**Rnd 12:** Work as for Rnd 10.

**Rnd 13:** *LT, k2 with color B, RT*; rep * to * around.

**Rnd 14:** With color B only, *K1, sl 1, k2, sl 1, k1*; rep * to * around.

**Rnd 15:** *K1 with color B, LT, RT, k1 with color B*; rep * to * around.

**Rnd 16:** With color B only, *K2, sl 2, k2*; rep * to * around.

Rep Rnds1–2 until cap measures 5¼ (6, 6¾, 7½) in [13 (15, 17, 19) cm].

### SHAPE CROWN

Change to dpn when sts no longer fit around circular.

**Rnd 1:** *K2 with color B, k2tog with color A, k2 with color B*; rep * to * around.

**Rnd 2:** K2 with color B, sl 1, k2 with color B*; rep * to * around.

**Rnd 3:** K2 with color B, k1 with color A, k2 with color B*; rep * to * around.

**Rnd 4:** K2 with color B, sl 1, k2 with color B*; rep * to * around.

**Rnd 5:** K2tog with color B, k1 with color A, k2 with color B*; rep * to * around.

**Rnd 6:** K1 with color B, sl 1, k2 with color B*; rep * to * around.

**Rnd 7:** K1 with color B, k1 with color A, k2tog with color B*; rep * to * around.

**Rnd 8:** K1 with color B, sl 1, k1 with color B*; rep * to * around.

**Rnd 9:** K1 with color B, k1 with color A, k1 with color B*; rep * to * around.

**Rnd 10:** K1 with color B, sl 1, k1 with color B*; rep * to * around.

**Rnd 11:** K2tog with color A, k1 with color B*; rep * to * around.

**Rnd 12:** *Sl 1, k1 with color B*; rep * to * around.

**Rnd 13:** *K1 with color A, k1 with color B*; rep * to * around.

**Rnd 14:** *K2tog tbl with color A*; rep * to * around.

**Rnd 15:** *K2tog tbl with color A*; rep * to * around, ending with k1 (0, 1, 0) tbl.

Cut yarn and draw end through rem sts; tighten.

### FINISHING

Weave in all ends neatly on WS.

Block cap by covering it with a damp towel; leave until completely dry or gently steam press under a damp pressing cloth but do not press ribbing.

If desired, securely attach a faux fur pom-pom.

Julie Turtleneck Pullover →»

# Julie Turtleneck Pullover

One of our first pullover patterns was the Julie pullover, a thin summer sweater knitted with alpaca/silk yarn. Now we've designed a heavier version in Spøt, with the same delicate lace pattern on the sleeves and a lovely high neck.

*Level 2*

**Sizes:** 6 months (1, 2, 4, 6, 8, 10) years

**FINISHED MEASUREMENTS**
Chest: Approx. 22½ (23¾, 24¼, 26¾, 27¼, 29, 29¾) in [57 (60, 61.5, 68, 69, 73.5, 75.5) cm]

Length: Approx. 11¾ (13, 14½, 16½, 18½, 19¾, 20½) in [30 (33, 37, 42, 47, 50, 52) cm]

**MATERIALS**
**Yarn:** Sandnes Garn KlompeLompe Spøt [CYCA #3 – DK, light worsted, 40% Merino wool, 40% alpaca, 20% nylon, 147 yd (134 m) / 50 g

**YARN COLORS AND AMOUNTS:**
Dusty Pink 4011: 150 (150, 200, 200, 250, 300, 300) g

**Needles:** U.S. sizes 2.5 and 4 (3 and 3.5 mm): 24 in (60 cm) circulars and sets of 5 dpn

**Gauge:** 22 sts in stockinette on larger size needles = 4 in (10 cm).

Adjust needle size to obtain correct gauge if necessary.

**PATTERN CHART: SEE PAGE 142.**
The sweater is worked top down.

With smaller size circular, CO 78 (80, 80, 82, 86, 86, 88) sts. Join, being careful not to twist cast-on row; pm for beginning of rnd. Work around in k1, p1 ribbing for 3¼ (4, 4¾, 5½, 5½, 6¼, 6¼) in [8 (10, 12, 14, 14, 16, 16) cm]. Change to larger size circular.

Knit 1 rnd, increasing 26 (24, 24, 30, 26, 34, 32) sts evenly spaced around = 104 (104, 104, 112, 112, 120, 120) sts. Pm to set off pattern sections: Pm, work 17 sts in pattern, pm, k35 (35, 35, 39, 39, 43, 43), pm, work 17 sts in pattern, pm, k35 (35, 35, 39, 39, 43, 43).

Now work in lace pattern (see chart on page 142) over the 17 sts at each side and in stockinette over rem sts.

Work 5 rnds as est.

On next rnd, increase 32 sts (all sizes) evenly spaced over stockinette sections (= increase 16 sts each over front and back).

Work 8 rnds as est.

On next rnd, increase 32 sts (all sizes) evenly spaced over stockinette sections (= increase 16 sts each over front and back).

**Sizes 4 (6, 8, 10) years:** Work 8 rnds as est.

On next rnd, increase 32 sts (all sizes) evenly spaced over stockinette sections (= increase 16 sts each over front and back).

**Sizes 8 (10) years:** Work 8 rnds as est.

On next rnd, increase 32 sts (all sizes) evenly spaced over stockinette sections (= increase 16 sts each over front and back).

**ALL SIZES:**
Knit 10 rnds.

On next rnd, increase 22 (32, 44, 22, 32, 14, 26) sts evenly spaced over stockinette sections (= increase 11 (16, 22, 11, 16, 7, 13) sts each over front and back) = 190 (200, 212, 230, 240, 262, 274) sts.

Work 3 rnds.

Cut yarn and slip the last 11 (12, 14, 15, 17, 20, 22) sts to left needle. The rnd now begins here.

Divide for body and sleeves:

Place the first 39 (41, 45, 47, 51, 57, 61) sts on a holder (sleeve), k56 (59, 61, 68, 69, 74, 76), place next 39 (41, 45, 47, 51, 57, 61) sts on a holder (sleeve), k56 (59, 61, 68, 69, 74, 76).

Place sts for front and back on same circular, but, at each underarm, CO 7 sts = a total of 126 (132, 136, 150, 152, 162, 166) sts. The st at center of each underarm is a marked (pm around st).

**FRONT AND BACK**
Knit in the round until body, from shoulders, measures 10¼ (11½, 13½, 14½, 16½, 17¼, 18¼) in [26 (29, 34, 37, 42, 44, 46) cm].

Change to smaller size circular and work in k1, p1 ribbing for 1½ (1½, 1½, 2, 2, 2½, 2½) in [4 (4, 4, 5, 5, 6, 6) cm]. BO in ribbing on last rnd.

**SLEEVES**
With larger size dpn, CO 4 sts, work the held 39 (41, 45, 47, 51, 57, 61) sleeve sts, CO 3 sts. You are now at the center of the underarm. Mark first st and always purl it. Work sleeve in the round.

Work as est for 1 in (2.5 cm) and then begin shaping sleeve: P1 (marked st), k2tog, work until 2 sts rem, sl 1, k1, psso.

Decrease the same way approx. every 1 (1, 1¼, 1⅜, 1⅜, 1, 1) in [2.5 (2.5, 3, 3.5, 3.5, 2.5, 2.5) cm] until 32 (34, 38, 40, 42, 42, 44) sts rem.

When sleeve is 7 (8, 9½, 11½, 12¼, 13¾, 15) in [18 (20, 24, 29, 31, 35, 38) cm] long (or desired length), change to smaller size dpn. Work around in k1, p1 ribbing for 1½ (1½, 1½, 2, 2, 2½, 2½) in [4 (4, 4, 5, 5, 6, 6) cm]. BO in ribbing on last rnd.

Make second sleeve the same way.

**FINISHING**
Weave in all ends neatly on WS.

Block sweater by covering it with a damp towel; leave until completely dry.

# Henry Felted Mittens

These mittens are felted but won't be too thick. They work especially nicely when paired with cozy liner mittens so the wind won't blow through them. The pattern is sized for both children and adults.

*Level 2*

**Sizes:** 1–2 (3–4, 5–7, 8–10 years, S/M, M/L adult)

**MATERIALS**
**Yarn:** Sandnes Garn Tove [CYCA #2 – sport, 100% wool, 175 yd (160 m) / 50 g]

**YARN COLORS AND AMOUNTS:**
Color A/MC: Dusty Purple 4342: 50 (50, 50, 50, 50, 50) g

Color B/CC: Light Gray Heather 1035: 50 (50, 50, 50, 50, 50) g

**Needles:** U.S. size 8 (5 mm): 32 in (80 cm) circular for magic loop or set of 5 dpn

**Gauge:** Before felting 18–19 sts in stockinette = 4 in (10 cm).

Adjust needle size to obtain correct gauge if necessary.

The round begins at the side.

With MC, CO 28 (28, 32, 36, 40, 44) sts. Divide sts onto dpn and join. Purl 1 rnd, knit 1 rnd, purl 1 rnd. Change to CC. Knit 1 rnd, purl 1 rnd. Change to MC and knit 1 rnd, purl 1 rnd.

Knit 1 rnd, increasing 2 (2, 4, 6, 2, 4) sts evenly spaced around = 30 (30, 36, 42, 42, 48) sts. Knit 2 rnds.

> **Knitting Tip:** We recommend twisting the yarns around each other when the floats are too long, so fingers won't catch in the long strands when pulling on the mittens.

Now work following chart all around.

After working 11 (13, 15, 16, 23, 23) rnds in charted pattern, work thumbhole:

**RIGHT-HAND MITTEN**
K1 in pattern, with smooth, contrasting color yarn, k6 (6, 7, 7, 7, 8) sts, slide the 6 (6, 7, 7, 7, 8) sts back to left needle and knit in pattern. Continue in pattern following chart to end of rnd.

**LEFT-HAND MITTEN**
K8 (8, 10, 13, 13, 15) in pattern, with smooth, contrasting color yarn, k6 (6, 7, 7, 7, 8) sts, slide the 6 (6, 7, 7, 7, 8) sts back to left needle and knit in pattern. Continue in pattern following chart to end of rnd.

Continue following charted pattern for 13 (14, 20, 24, 24, 28) rnds.

Pm at each side.

Work with only MC, shaping top as follows:

*Sl 1, k1, psso, knit until 2 st before marker, k2tog*; rep * to * once more = 4 sts decreased.

Decrease the same way on every other rnd a total of 2 times and then decrease on every rnd until 6 (6, 6, 6, 6, 8) sts rem. Cut yarn and draw end through rem sts; tighten.

### THUMB

Insert 1 dpn though 6 (6, 7, 7, 7, 8) sts below waste yarn and another dpn through 6 (6, 7, 7, 7, 8) sts above waste yarn. Carefully remove waste yarn. Divide sts onto 3 dpn and, with MC, knit around on these 12 (12, 14, 14, 14 16) sts for 1⅝ (1¾, 2, 2½, 2¾, 3¼) in [4 (4.5, 5, 6, 7, 8) cm]. K2tog around. Cut yarn and draw end through rem sts; tighten.

### FELTING

Wash mittens separately with normal laundry soap on regular setting at 104°F (40°C). Shape mittens while they are wet and lay them flat to dry. If you want smaller mittens, you can scrub them on a felting board until they are desired size.

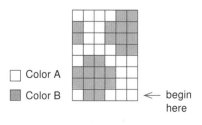

☐ Color A
▨ Color B    ← begin here

**Accessory Tip:** We wrapped yarn around the Nerigjønå cowl to transform it into a headband.

# Dottie Deer Pullover

Winter's sweetest sweater. Dottie, who is perhaps a cross between Bambi and Rudolph, is a children's favorite. The sweater is fun to knit and has embroidered details that take a little time but are well worth it.

*Level 3*

**Sizes:** 1 (2, 4, 6, 8, 10 years)

**FINISHED MEASUREMENTS**
Chest: Approx. 21¼ (22, 24½, 27¾, 29½, 30¼) in [54 (56, 62, 70.5, 75, 77) cm]

Total Length: Approx. 12¾ (14¼, 16¼, 18, 19, 21¼) in [32 (36, 41, 45.5, 48.5, 54) cm]

**MATERIALS**
**Yarn:** Sandnes Garn KlompeLompe Tynn Merinoull (fine Merino wool) [CYCA #1 – fingering, 100% Merino wool, 191 yd (175 m) / 50 g]

**YARN COLORS AND AMOUNTS:**
Color A: Powder Pink 4344: 50 (50 (50) 50 (50) 100) g

Color B: Powder Rose 4032: 100 (150, 150, 150, 200, 250) g

Color C: Putty 1013: 50 (50, 50, 50, 50, 50) g

Color D: Gray-Brown 2652: 50 (50, 50, 50, 50, 50) g

+ small amounts for deer face

**Needles:** U.S. sizes 1.5 and 2.5 (2.5 and 3 mm): 16 and 24 in (40 and 60 cm) circulars and sets of 5 dpn

**Gauge:** 27 sts on larger size needles = 4 in (10 cm).

Adjust needle size to obtain correct gauge if necessary.

The sweater is worked from the top down, in the round, on circular needles.

With color A and smaller size circular, CO 90 (94, 100, 100, 108, 114) sts. Join, being careful not to twist cast-on row; pm for beginning of rnd. Work around in k1, p1 ribbing for 1¼ (1¼, 1¼, 1⅜, 1⅜, 1⅜) in [3 (3, 3.5, 3.5. 3.5) cm].

Change to larger size circular and knit 1 rnd.

Knit 1 rnd, increasing 50 (60, 54, 68, 60, 68) sts evenly spaced around = 140 (154, 154, 168, 168, 182) sts.

Now work following pattern chart A.

After completing chart rows, there should be 220 (242, 242, 264, 264, 286) sts.

Knit 0 (0, 0, 4, 4, 4) rnds with color B. Knit 1 rnd, increasing 0 (0, 0, 40, 56, 34) sts evenly spaced around = 220 (242, 242, 304, 320, 320) sts.

With color B, knit 0 (2, 1, 3, 6, 6) rnds. Knit 1 rnd, increasing 26 (16, 36, 0, 0, 12) sts evenly spaced around = 246 (258, 278, 304, 320, 332) sts.

**Size 4 years:** Knit 4 rnds.

**Sizes 8 (10) years:** Knit 4 (6) rnds.

**DIVIDE FOR BODY AND SLEEVES**
Place the next 56 (60, 62, 64, 66, 69) sts on a holder (sleeve), CO 7 sts for underarm, k67 (69, 77, 88, 94, 97) (front), place the next 56 (60, 62, 64, 66, 69) sts on a holder (sleeve), CO 7 sts for underarm, k67 (69, 77, 88, 94, 97) (back).

## FRONT AND BACK
There are 148 (152, 168, 190, 202, 208) sts for body.

With color B, work around in stockinette until body measures 9½ (11½, 13, 14½, 15¾, 17¾) in [24 (29, 33, 37, 40, 45) cm].

Knit 1 rnd, decreasing 0 (0, 0, 1, 1, 0) st at each side = 0 (0, 0, 2, 2, 0) sts decreased.

Work following chart B.

With color A, knit 1 rnd.

Change to smaller size circular and work in k1, p1 ribbing for 1¼ (1¼, 1¼, 1⅜, 1⅜, 1½) in [3 (3, 3, 3.5, 3.5. 4) cm]. BO in ribbing on last rnd.

## SLEEVES
With color B and larger size dpn, CO 4 sts, k56 (60, 62, 64, 66, 69) held sts, CO 3 sts, pm.

Work in the round. The first st is a marked st and always purled.

When sleeve is ¾ in (2) cm long, begin shaping as follows:

Knit until 2 sts before marker, sl 1, k1, psso, sl m, p1 (marked st), k2tog.

Decrease the same way every ⅝ (¾, ¾, 1, 1, 1⅜) in [1.5 (2, 2, 2.5, 2.5, 3.5) cm] until 49 (53, 53, 53, 53, 60) sts rem.

When sleeve measures 5¼ (6¼, 7½, 9, 10¾, 12¾) in [13 (16, 19, 23, 27, 32) cm], knit 1 rnd, decreasing 1 (1, 1, 1, 1, 0) st.

Now work following chart B. Knit 1 rnd with color A, decreasing 2 (4, 4, 2, 2, 6) sts evenly spaced round.

Change to smaller size dpn and work around in k1, p1 ribbing for 1¼ (1¼, 1¼, 1⅜, 1⅜, 1½) in [3 (3, 3, 3.5, 3.5. 4) cm]. BO in ribbing on last rnd.

## FINISHING
Weave in all ends neatly on WS.

With double strand of yarn, embroider nose on each deer. Use a single strand to embroider rem features.

Block sweater by covering it with a damp towel; leave until completely dry.

Chart A

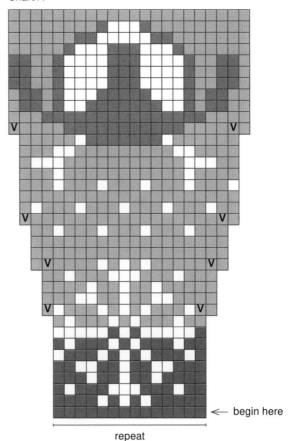

← begin here

repeat

Chart B

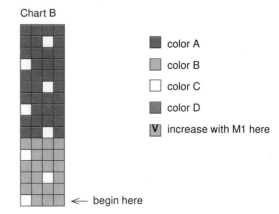

← begin here

■ color A
■ color B
□ color C
■ color D
V increase with M1 here

# Little Troll Pants

Our well-known little troll pattern appears here on these sweet pants. The texture pattern makes the pants nicely warm around the body while the stockinette-knit legs allow for easy movement.

*Level 2*

---

**Sizes:** 0–1 (3–6, 9–12, 18 months, 2, 4 years)

**FINISHED MEASUREMENTS**
Waist: Approx. 19¼ (19¼, 21, 21, 22¼, 22¼) in [49 (49, 53, 53, 56.5, 56.5) cm]

Total Leg Length: Approx. 6¼ (7, 9¾, 11, 11¾, 13) in [16, 18, 25, 28, 30, 33) cm]

**MATERIALS**
**Yarn:** Sandnes Garn KlompeLompe Merinoull [CYCA #3 – DK, light worsted, 100% Merino wool, 114 yd (104 m) / 50 g]

**YARN COLORS AND AMOUNTS:**
Gray-Brown 2652: 150 (200, 250, 300, 300, 350) g

**Needles:** U.S. sizes 2.5 and 4 (3 and 3.5 mm): 16 and 24 in (40 and 60 cm) circulars and sets of 5 dpn

**Crochet Hook:** U.S. size C-2 (2.5 mm)

**Notions:** 2 buttons

**Gauge:** 22 sts on larger size needles = 4 in (10 cm).

Adjust needle size to obtain correct gauge if necessary.

---

The pants are worked top down.

With smaller size circular, CO 108 (108, 116, 116, 124, 124) sts. Join, being careful not to twist cast-on row; pm for beginning of rnd. Work around in k1, p1 ribbing for 13 (13, 15, 15, 17, 17) rnds, **but**, on the 6th (6th, 7th, 7th, 8th, 8th) rnd, make 2 buttonholes at the front. Work 43 (43, 46, 46, 48, 48) sts in ribbing, BO 2 sts, work 18 (18, 20, 20, 24, 24) sts in ribbing, BO 2 sts, work 43 (43, 46, 46, 48, 48) sts in ribbing. On next rnd, CO 2 sts over each gap.

Change to larger size needle, Knit 1 rnd, increasing 6 (12, 10, 16, 14, 20) sts evenly spaced around = 114 (120, 126, 132, 138, 144) sts.

Now raise back with short rows.

**Note:** There is a yarnover after each turn; when you later come to one, knit/purl the yarnover with next st).

K10; turn, yo. P20; turn, yo. K25; turn, yo. P30; turn, yo. K35; turn, yo. P40; turn, yo. K20. You are now back at beginning of rnd.

Begin working in texture pattern:

**Rnd 1:** *Sl 3 st purlwise wyf, p3*; rep * to * around.

**Rnd 2:** Work as for Rnd 1.

**Rnds 3–5:** Knit.

**Rnd 6:** K1, *K1 tog with the 2 strands from Rnds 1 and 2, k5*; rep * to * around until 5 sts rem, k1 tog with the 2 strands from Rnds 1 and 2, k4.

**Rnd 7:** *P3, sl 3 st purlwise wyf*; rep * to * around.

**Rnd 8:** Work as for Rnd 7.

**Rnds 9–11:** Knit.

**Rnd 12:** K4, *K1 tog with the 2 strands from Rnds 7 and 8, k5*; rep * to * around until 2 sts rem, k1 tog with the 2 strands from Rnds 7 and 8, k1.

Rep Rnds 1–12.

Continue in pattern until body measures 8¼ (10¼, 11½, 12¼, 13, 13¾) in [21 (26, 29, 31, 33, 35) cm] down front of pants and the next rnd is 6 or 12 in pattern.

On the next rnd, decrease as follows: BO 3 sts, work 51 (54, 57, 60, 63, 66) sts in pattern, BO 6 sts, work 51 (54, 57, 60, 63, 66) sts in pattern, BO 3 sts.

Work each leg separately = 51 (54, 57, 60, 63, 66) sts for each leg. Pm for beginning of rnd. Work 12 rnds in pattern.

Change to stockinette. After working for ⅜ in (1 cm), begin shaping leg as follows: K1, k2tog, knit until 3 sts rem, sl 1, k1, psso, k1. Decrease the same way every ⅜ (¾, 1½, 2, 2½, 2¾) in [1 (2, 4, 5, 6, 7) cm] a total of 3 times. Continue in stockinette until leg measures 4¼ (5¼, 8, 9, 9¾, 11) in [11 (13, 20, 23, 25, 28) cm]. Work 12 rnds in pattern. Knit 1 rnd, decreasing 7 (10, 9, 12, 13, 16) sts evenly spaced around = 38 (38, 42, 42, 44, 44) sts rem.

Change to smaller size dpn. Work 20 rnds in k1, p1 ribbing. BO in ribbing on last rnd.

Make second leg the same way.

Make an I-cord (see video at klompelompe.no). With larger size dpn, CO 4 sts. Knit the sts. *Do not turn. Slide the sts back to front of needle, bring yarn across WS, and knit the sts.* Rep from * to * until cord is approx. 17¼ (19, 20½, 22, 23¾, 25¼) in [44 (48, 52, 56, 60, 64) cm] long. Make second I-cord the same way.

Sew the center of the cord securely at center back of pants. Crochet a button loop at each end of the cord: ch 6, attach chain with sl st (measure to make sure chain is long enough for button. Sew a button to the cord approx. 2½ in (6 cm) from the end. Bring the cord through the buttonhole from back to front. Attach second cord the same way.

**FINISHING**
Weave in all ends neatly on WS.

Block pants by covering with a damp towel; leave until completely dry.

# Izzy Cap

A two-color pattern cap that can be enhanced with a faux fur pom-pom.

*Level 2*

--------------------------------

**Sizes:** 1–2 (3– 4, 5–7, 8–10) years

**MATERIALS**
**Yarn:** Sandnes Garn KlompeLompe Spøt [CYCA #3 – DK, light worsted, 40% Merino wool, 40% alpaca, 20% nylon, 147 yd (134 m) / 50 g]

**YARN COLORS AND AMOUNTS:**
Color A: Putty 1013: 50 (50, 50, 50) g

Color B: Light Flax Blue 6041: 50 (50, 50, 50) g

**Needles:** U.S. sizes 2.5 and 6 (3 and 4 mm): 16 in (40 cm) circulars and set of 5 dpn in larger size.

**Gauge:** 22 sts in stockinette on larger size needles = 4 in (10 cm).

Adjust needle size to obtain correct gauge if necessary.

--------------------------------

With smaller size circular and color A, CO 80 (85, 90, 90) sts. Join, being careful not to twist cast-on row; pm for beginning of rnd. Work 10 rnds in k1, p1 ribbing.

Change to larger size circular and color B. Knit 1 rnd, increasing 10 (15, 15, 20) sts evenly spaced around = 90 (100, 105, 110) sts.

Work following chart until cap measures 6 (6¾, 7, 8) in [15 (17, 18, 20) cm].

Knit 1 rnd with color B, decreasing 2 (4, 1, 6) sts evenly spaced around.

**SHAPE CROWN**
Change to dpn when sts no longer fit around circular.

Continue with color B.

**Decrease Rnd 1:** *K6, k2tog*; rep * to * around. Knit 2 rnds.

**Decrease Rnd 2:** *K5, k2tog*; rep * to * around. Knit 2 rnds.

**Decrease Rnd 3:** *K4, k2tog*; rep * to * around. Knit 2 rnds.

**Decrease Rnd 4:** *K3, k2tog*; rep * to * around.

**Decrease Rnd 5:** *K6, k2tog*; rep * to * around, ending with k4 (0, 4, 4).

**Decrease Rnd 6:** *K5, k2tog*; rep * to * around, ending with k4 (0, 4, 4).

**Decrease Rnd 7:** *K4, k2tog*; rep * to * around, ending with k4 (0, 4, 4).

**Decrease Rnd 8:** *K3, k2tog*; rep * to * around, ending with k4 (0, 4, 4).

**Decrease Rnd 9:** *K2, k2tog*; rep * to * around.

**Decrease Rnd 10:** *K2tog*; rep * to * around, ending with k0 (0, 1, 1).

Cut yarn and draw end through rem sts; tighten.

**FINISHING**
Weave in all ends neatly on WS.

Block cap by covering it with a damp towel; leave until completely dry.

Securely attach a faux fur pom-pom to top of cap if desired.

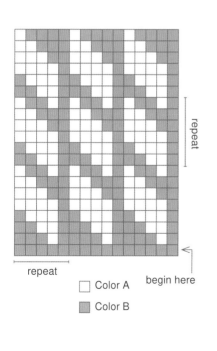

Color A

Color B

repeat

repeat

begin here

**Knitting Tip:** We knitted this cap and the matching sweater with needles U.S. 6 (4 mm) because the stranded colorwork pattern can easily draw in, making the cap too tight. Use the needle size you need to ensure that you have the correct gauge.

# Izzy Polar Bear Pullover

When we thought about winter, the first thing that popped into our minds was a polar bear. This sweater pattern knits up quickly. You can knit it without the polar bear motif if the recipient thinks they're too grown up for that.

## Level 2

**Sizes:** 1 (2, 4, 6, 8, 10) years

### FINISHED MEASUREMENTS

Chest: Approx. 23¼ (24, 25¼, 25¾, 28¾, 30¼) in [59 (61, 64, 65.5, 73, 77) cm]

Total Length: Approx. 13½ (15, 16¼, 18¼, 19¾, 21¾) in [34 (38, 41, 46, 50, 55) cm]

### MATERIALS

**Yarn:** Sandnes Garn KlompeLompe Spøt [CYCA #3 – DK, light worsted, 40% Merino wool, 40% alpaca, 20% nylon, 147 yd (134 m) / 50 g]

### YARN COLORS AND AMOUNTS:

Color A: Putty 1013: 100 (150, 150, 150, 200, 200) g

Color B: Light Flax Blue 6041: 100 (100, 100, 150, 150, 150) g

+ small amounts for polar bear features

**Needles:** U.S. sizes 2.5 and 6 (3 and 4 mm): 16 and 14 in (40 and 60 cm) circulars or 32 in (80 cm) circular for magic loop and sets of 5 dpn

**Gauge:** 22 sts in stockinette on larger size needles = 4 in (10 cm).

Adjust needle size to obtain correct gauge if necessary.

The pullover is worked from the bottom up, with the round beginning at the side.

With smaller size circular and color A, CO 130 (134, 140, 144, 160, 170) sts. Join, being careful not to twist cast-on row; pm for beginning of rnd. Work around in k1, p1 ribbing for 1¼ (1¼, 1⅜, 1⅜, 1½, 1½) in [3 (3, 3.5, 3.5, 4, 4) cm]. Change to larger size circular. Work following chart. On first rnd working from chart, increase 0 (1, 0, 1, 0, 0) st. Continue in charted pattern until sweater measures 8¼ (9½, 10¼, 11¾, 13, 14¼) in [21 (24, 26, 30, 33, 36) cm]. On next rnd, BO 6 sts centered on each side.

### SLEEVES

With smaller size dpn and color A, CO 36 (36, 38, 38, 40, 40) sts. Divide sts onto dpn and join. Work around in k1, p1 ribbing for 1¼ (1¼, 1⅜, 1⅜, 1½, 1½) in [3 (3, 3.5, 3.5, 4, 4) cm]. Change to larger size dpn. The first st of rnd is a marked st for center of underarm. Always purl marked st with color B. Work following chart. On first rnd working from chart, increase 4 (4, 2, 2, 5, 5) sts evenly spaced around = 40 (40, 40, 40, 45, 45) sts.

Continue in pattern until sleeve measures 9½ (11, 12¼, 13½, 14¼, 15) in [24 (28, 31, 34, 36, 38) cm], **but**, after ¾ in (2 cm), increase as follows: p1, M1, knit to end of rnd, M1.

Increase the same way every 1⅜ in (3.5 cm) until there are 50 (52, 54, 56, 59, 63) sts and sleeve measures 9½ (11,

12¼, 13½, 14¼, 15) in [24 (28, 31, 34, 36, 38) cm]. BO 6 sts centered on underarm. Set sleeve aside while you knit second sleeve the same way.

### YOKE

Arrange sleeves with body on larger size circular, matching underarms. Place marker 1 at left sleeve, marker 2 at front, marker 3 at right sleeve, and marker 4 at back = 206 (214, 224, 232, 254, 272) sts and 4 markers.

The 2 sts before and the 2 sts after each marker are raglan sts and are always knitted with color A = 4 raglan sts at each marker.

Knit 1 rnd, with color A at each 4-st raglan line and in pattern for rem sts.

On next rnd, decrease as follows: *K1, sl 1, k1 with color A, psso, knit until 3 sts before next marker, k2tog with color A, k1*; rep * to * around = 8 sts decreased.

Decrease the same way on every other rnd a total of 16 (17, 18, 19, 21, 23) times = 78 (78, 80, 80, 86, 88) sts rem.

Raise back with short rows (continuing in pattern and color A raglan lines):

Knit to marker 2; turn, sl first st, purl to marker 3; turn, sl first st. Knit to marker 1; turn, sl first st, purl to marker 4; turn, sl first st. Knit to marker 1 (beginning of rnd). Change to smaller size circular and, with color A, knit 1 rnd. With color A, work 18 (18, 18, 18, 20, 20) rnds, k1, p1 ribbing. BO in ribbing on last rnd.

### FINISHING

Seam underarms.

Fold neckband in half and sew down on WS with color A.

Weave in all ends neatly on WS.

Block sweater by covering it with a damp towel; leave until completely dry.

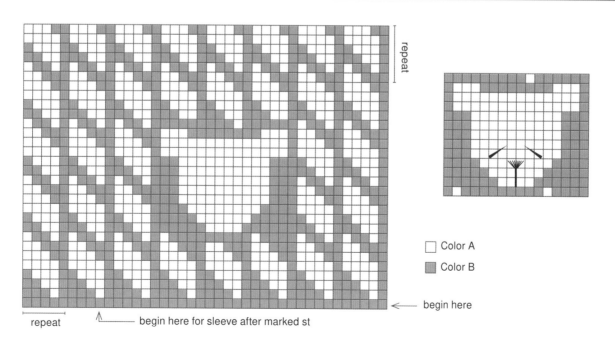

repeat

begin here

repeat

↑ begin here for sleeve after marked st

☐ Color A

▨ Color B

107

# Kari Coat

A simple silhouette, a back pleat, and fine button details make this coat a must-have in the knitted wardrobe. And how fun it is to make a beautiful coat yourself.

*Level 3*

- - - - - - - - - - - - - - - - - - - - - - - - -

**Sizes:** 12 (18 months, 2, 4, 6, 8, 10 years)

**FINISHED MEASUREMENTS**
Chest: Approx. 19¾ (20½, 21¼, 22¾, 24½, 26¾, 28) in [50 (52, 54, 58, 62.5, 68, 71.5) cm]

Total Length: Approx. 14½ (15, 15¾, 18¼, 20, 21¼, 23¾) in [37 (38, 40, 46, 51, 54, 60) cm]

**MATERIALS**
**Yarn:** Sandnes Garn KlompeLompe Merinoull [CYCA #3 – DK, light worsted, 100% Merino wool, 114 yd (104 m) / 50 g]

**YARN COLORS AND AMOUNTS:**
Powder Rose 4032: 250 (250, 300, 350, 400, 400, 450) g

**Needles:** U.S. sizes 2.5 and 6 (3 and 4 mm): 16 and 24 in (40 and 60 cm) circulars or 32 in (80 cm) circular for magic loop and sets of 5 dpn

**Notions:** 6 buttons (all sizes)

**Gauge:** 22 sts in stockinette on larger size needles = 4 in (10 cm).

Adjust needle size to obtain correct gauge if necessary.

- - - - - - - - - - - - - - - - - - - - - - - - -

The coat is worked from the bottom up, back and forth, on a circular needle.

With larger size circular, CO 164 (168, 172, 182, 192, 212, 220) sts. Knit 16 rows = 8 garter ridges.

On next (RS) row, continue in garter st on the first 10 and last 10 sts. Work rerm sts in garter st (knit on RS, purl on WS).

Continue as est until piece measures 6 in (15 cm) (all sizes). On next RS row, pm as follows:

K35 (36, 37, 40, 42, 46, 48), pm, k33 (34, 35, 37, 40, 46, 48), pm, k28, pm, k33 (34, 35, 37, 40, 46, 48), pm, k35 (36, 37, 40, 42, 46, 48).

On next RS row, decrease as follows:

*Knit until 2 sts before marker, sl 1, k1, psso, k2tog*; rep * to * at each marker = 8 sts decreased.

Decrease the same way every 1½ (1, 2½, 3¼, 4, 3, 3½) in [4 (5, 6, 8.5, 10, 7.5, 9) cm].

After decreasing a total of 3 (3, 3, 3, 3, 4, 4) times, and, when next row is RS, make a pleat:

Knit until 5 (5, 5, 5, 5, 6, 6) sts before 2nd marker, place the next 5 sts on a cable needle (= cable needle 1), place next 5 sts on a cable needle (= cable needle 2). Arrange cable needle 1, cable needle 2, and left needle over each other to form a Z. *K3tog (with 1 st each from cable needle 1, cable needle 2, left needle)*; rep * to * 5 times. K2. Place sts on

cable needles as before, but arrange the needles over each other as for a reversed Z. K3tog 5 times as before. Knit to end of row = 120 (124, 128, 138, 148, 160, 168) sts.

Work 3 rows.

**Next Row (RS):** K27 (28, 29, 32, 34, 37, 40), BO 8 sts, k50 (52, 54, 58, 64, 70, 72), BO 8 sts, k27 (28, 29, 32, 34, 37, 40). Set body aside while you knit sleeves.

## SLEEVES
With smaller size dpn, CO 34 (36, 36, 38, 40, 40, 42) sts. Divide sts onto dpn and join. Work 5 garter ridges (1 ridge = purl 1 rnd, knit 1 rnd). Change to larger size dpn and stockinette. After 1½ in (4 cm) increase: *K1, M1, knit until 1 st rem, M1, k1.*

Rep * to * every 1 (1, 1¼, 1½, 1½, 2, 2) in [2.5 (2.5, 3, 4, 4, 5, 5) cm] = 48 (50, 50, 52, 54, 54, 56) sts.

Continue in stockinette until sleeve measures 8 (8¾, 9½, 11½, 12¼, 13¾, 15) in [20 (22, 24, 29, 31, 35, 38) cm]. The sleeves are shorter than normal because the yoke is long. BO 8 sts centered on underarm = 40 (42, 42, 44, 46, 46, 48) sts rem.

Set sleeve aside while you knit second sleeve the same way.

## YOKE
Arrange sleeves with body on larger size circular, matching underarms = 184 (192, 196, 210, 224, 236, 248) sts total.

Pm 1 st in on body at each intersection of body and sleeve = 4 markers.

On every RS row, decrease as follows:

*Knit to marker, sl 1, k1, psso. Knit until 2 sts before next marker, k2tog*; rep * to *.

On the 2nd decrease row, make 2 buttonholes:

K2, BO 2 sts, k3, BO 2 sts, k1, work to end of row, decreasing at markers as est.

On next row, CO 2 sts over each gap.

Make 2 more buttonholes placed as before on the 8th (9th, 9th, 9th, 10th, 10th, 10th) decrease row.

On the 11th (12th, 12th, 12th, 13th, 13th, 13th) decrease row and every subsequent RS row, shape neck: K2tog at beginning and end of row. The garter sts at each side will gradually be eliminated.

On the 16th (17th, 17th, 18th, 19th, 19th, 20th) decrease row, BO 10 sts at center back.

Now work each side separately. Continue on left side and place right side sts on a holder.

Begin decreasing at raglan markers on both RS and WS rows, but, at front and back necks only on RS rows.

On WS, decrease at markers as:

First marker, p2tog

Other markers: Sl 2 knitwise, one at a time. Place sts back on left needle and p2tog.

On RS, decrease at markers as before and k2tog at beginning and end of row.

After 4 rows, pm at center of sleeve (centered between the 2 markers) and remove previous markers.

Decrease on each side of marker on each row and decrease as before on RS at each end.

Now shape shoulder.

After working 5 (5, 5, 5, 5, 7, 7) rows and moving markers, and the next row is on RS, work as before, but, at the same time. BO. Join shoulders with Kitchener st (see page 7).

## COLLAR
**Note:** After a turn, slip the first st and tighten yarn slightly.

Pick up and knit sts for collar on WS, with 1 st in each st. Pm at each shoulder.

Purl 1 row.

**Short Row 1:** Knit until 1 st rem; turn.

**Short Row 2:** Purl until 1 st rem; turn.

**Short Row 3:** Knit until 1 st before previous turn, and, *at the same time*, increase 10 sts evenly spaced across back; turn.

**Short Row 4:** Purl until 1 st before previous turn; turn.

**Short Row 5:** Knit until 1 st before previous turn; turn.

**Short Row 6:** Purl until 1 st before previous turn; turn.

**Short Row 7:** Knit until 1 st before previous turn; turn.

**Short Row 8:** Purl until 1 st before previous turn; turn.

**Short Row 9:** Knit until 3 sts before previous turn; turn.

**Short Row 10:** Purl until 3 sts before previous turn; turn.

**Short Row 11:** Knit until 3 sts before previous turn, and, *at the same time*, increase 5 sts evenly spaced across back; turn.

**Short Row 12:** Purl until 3 sts before previous turn; turn.

**Short Row 13:** Knit until 3 sts before previous turn; turn.

**Short Row 14:** Purl until 3 sts before previous turn; turn.

**SIZES 6 (8, 10) YEARS:**
**Short Row 15:** Knit until 3 sts before previous turn; turn.

**Short Row 16:** Purl until 3 sts before previous turn; turn.

**ALL SIZES:**
**Next Row:** Knit to end of row.

Knit 3 rows, binding off on last row.

**FINISHING**
Weave in all ends neatly on WS.

Sew on buttons.

Fold collar down and tack it down with a few loose sts.

Block coat by covering it with a damp towel; leave until completely dry.

Winter
Sweet Skirt →

# Winter Sweet Skirt

An unbelievably easy skirt to knit. The sewn-on fabric straps also make it an eye-catching project.

## Level 1

**Sizes:** Doll one size (child 1, 2, 4, 6, 8, 10 years)

### FINISHED MEASUREMENTS
Waist: Approx. 12¾ (18, 18½, 19¼, 19¾, 19¾, 20) in [32 (45.5, 47, 49, 50, 50, 51) cm]

Total Length: Approx. 11¾ (8¾, 9¼, 9¾, 12¼, 13½, 15½) in [12 (22.5, 23.5, 25, 31, 34.5, 39.5) cm]

### MATERIALS
**Yarn:** Sandnes Garn KlompeLompe Merinoull [CYCA #3 – DK, light worsted, 100% Merino wool, 114 yd (104 m) / 50 g]

### YARN COLORS AND AMOUNTS:
Powder Rose 4032: 50 (100, 150, 150, 200, 200, 250) g

**Needles:** U.S. sizes 2.5 and 6 (3 and 4 mm): 16 and 24 in (40 and 60 cm) circulars (the longer circular is needed for larger size only)

**Notions:** fabric, approx. 18¼ (31½, 33½, 35½, 38½, 41¼, 45¼) in 46 (80, 85, 90, 98, 105, 115) cm] long and 6¼ (8½, 8½, 8½, 10¼, 10¼, 10¼) in [16 (22, 22, 22, 26 26, 26) cm] wide + seam allowance on all sides; sewing thread to match fabric and yarn.

**Gauge:** 22 sts in stockinette on larger size needles = 4 in (10 cm).

Adjust needle size to obtain correct gauge if necessary.

The skirt is worked from the top down in the round on a circular needle. The round begins at center back.

With smaller size circular, CO 70 (100, 104, 108, 110, 110, 112) sts. Join, being careful not to twist cast-on row; pm for beginning of rnd. Work 10 (18, 18, 20, 20, 22, 22) rnds k1, p1 ribbing, **but**, on the 5th (11th, 11th, 11th, 11th, 11th, 11th) rnd, make 2 eyelets as follows: Work 3 (6, 6, 6, 6, 6, 6) sts in ribbing, BO 2 sts, rib until 5 (8, 8, 8, 8, 8, 8) sts rem, BO 2 sts, rib 3 (6, 6, 6, 6, 6, 6). On next rnd, CO 2 sts over each gap.

Change to larger size circular and knit 1 rnd. Knit 1 rnd, increasing 14 (40, 40, 40, 44, 44, 48) sts evenly spaced around = 84 (140, 144, 148, 154, 154, 160) sts.

Work around in stockinette for 1¼ (2, 2, 2, 2, 2, 2) in [3 (5, 5, 5, 5, 5, 5) cm]. Knit 1 rnd, increasing 14 (40, 40, 40, 44, 44, 48) sts evenly spaced around = 98 (180, 184, 188, 198, 198, 108) sts.

Work around in stockinette for 0 (2, 2½, 2½, 2¾, 2¾, 4) in [0 (5, 6, 6, 7, 7, 10) cm]. Knit 1 rnd, increasing 0 (20, 20, 20, 22, 22, 24) sts evenly spaced around = 98 (200, 204, 208, 220, 220, 232) sts.

Work around in stockinette for 1½ (1¼, 1¼, 1½, 3½, 4¾, 5½) in [4 (3, 3, 4, 9, 12, 14) cm]. Work 5 ridges in garter st (1 garter ridge = knit 1 rnd, purl 1 rnd). BO on last purl rnd.

## FINISHING

Weave in all ends neatly on WS.

Block skirt by covering it with a damp towel; leave until completely dry.

### SEWN STRAPS:

Sew two straps approx. 18¼ (31½, 33½, 35½, 38½, 41¼, 45¼) in [46 (80, 85, 90, 98, 105, 115) cm] long. Cut two fabric strips, each 3¼ (4¼, 4¼, 4¼, 5¼, 5¼, 5¼) in [8 (11, 11, 11, 13, 13, 13) cm] wide. Fold each strip with RS facing RS and sew a simple seam all down the long side. Sew a diagonal line on one end and cut away any excess fabric. Zigzag stitch over all the cut edges. Turn strap right side out and sew a simple seam and zigzag the open end. Baste a few stitches on the end and gather in the strap a bit. Sew strap securely to front of skirt with sewing thread in same color as yarn. There should be approx. 8 (14, 16, 16, 18, 20, 22) sts between the straps at center front.

Cross the straps on the back and thread them through the two eyelets on the back from inside the skirt. Tie into a bow.

# Fluffy Bobble Pullover

The softest, lightest pullover you can imagine. We love how it feels, and the pretty Merino wool bobbles enhance the overall look.

*Level 2*

**Sizes:** 1 (2, 4, 6, 8, 10) years

**FINISHED MEASUREMENTS**

Chest: Approx. 23¾ (24½, 27½, 28, 28, 30) in [60 (62.5, 70, 71, 71, 76) cm]

Total Length: Approx. 12¾ (14¼, 16¼, 17¼, 19, 20½) in [32 (36, 41, 44, 48, 52) cm]

**MATERIALS**

**Yarn:** Sandnes Garn Børstet Alpakka (Brushed Alpaca) (CYCA #5 – bulky, 96% alpaca, 4% nylon, 120 yd (110 m) / 50 g)

Sandnes Garn KlompeLompe Merinoull [CYCA #3 – DK, light worsted, 100% Merino wool, 114 yd (104 m) / 50 g]

**YARN COLORS AND AMOUNTS:**

MC: Brushed Alpaca: Gray Heather 1042: 100 (150, 150, 200, 200, 200) g

CC: Merinoull, Powder Pink 4344: 50 (50, 50, 50, 50, 50) g or leftovers

**Needles:** U.S. size 8 (5 mm): 16 and 24 in (40 and 60 cm) circulars and set of 5 dpn; optional: 32 in (80 cm) circular for magic loop

**Gauge:** 16 sts in stockinette = 4 in (10 cm).

Adjust needle size to obtain correct gauge if necessary.

The bobbles are worked with Merinoull: *K1, p1, k1* in next st (= 3 sts into 1); turn, p3; turn, k3; turn, p2tog, p1; turn, k2tog.

The sweater is worked top down with Brushed Alpaca.

With Brushed Alpaca and circular, CO 54 (56, 60, 62, 64, 66) sts. Join, being careful not to twist cast-on row, pm for beginning of rnd. Work 8 rnds k1, p1 ribbing.

Knit 1 rnd, increasing 10 sts evenly spaced around = 64 (66, 70, 72, 74, 76) sts.

Knit 2 (2, 3, 3, 4, 4) rnds.

Knit 1 rnd, increasing 24 (22, 26, 24, 22, 28) sts evenly spaced around = 88 (88, 96, 96, 96, 104) sts.

Knit 1 rnd.

**Next Rnd (bobbles):** Knit with MC , working bobbles with CC as follows:

K1, bobble, *k3, bobble*; rep * to * around until 2 sts rem, k2.

Knit 3 rnds.

**Next Rnd (increase):** K1, M1, *k2, M1*; rep * to * around until 1 st rem, k1 = 132 (132, 144, 144, 144, 156) sts.

Knit 1 (1, 2, 2, 3, 3) rnds.

**Next Rnd (bobbles):** *K5, bobble*; rep * to * around.

118

Knit 5 (5, 6, 6, 7, 7) rnds.

**Next Rnd (bobbles):** K8, bobble, *k11, bobble*; rep * to * around until 3 sts rem, k3.

Knit 1 rnd.

Knit 1 rnd, increasing 8 (20, 20, 26, 30, 30) sts evenly spaced around = 140 (152, 164, 170, 174, 186) sts.

Knit 0 (2, 3, 5, 7, 9) rnds.

On next rnd, divide for body and sleeves:

K40 (42, 48, 49, 49, 53), place next 30 (34, 34, 36, 38, 40) sts on a holder for sleeve, CO 8 sts for underarm, k40 (42, 48, 49, 49, 53), place next 30 (34, 34, 36, 38, 40) sts on a holder for sleeve, CO 8 sts for underarm = 96 (100, 112, 114, 114, 122) sts rem for body.

Work around in stockinette with Brushed Alpaca until body measures 10¾ (12¼, 14¼, 15½, 17, 18½) in [27 (31, 36, 39, 43, 47) cm]. Finish with k1, p1 ribbing for 2 in (5 cm). BO in ribbing on last rnd.

### SLEEVES

Beginning at center of underarm, with dpn or magic loop circular, pick up and knit 4 sts, With dpn, pick up held 30 (34, 34, 36, 38, 40) sts for sleeve, pick up and knit 4 sts on underarm. You are now at center of underarm – pm for beginning of rnd.

Knit around in stockinette until sleeve measures 6¼ (8, 8¾, 10¼, 11½, 12¾) in [16 (20, 22, 26, 29, 32) cm], **but**, when sleeve is 1¼ in (3 cm) long, begin shaping: K1, k2tog, knit until 3 sts rem, k2tog, k1.

Decrease the same way every 1¼ (1¼, 1⅜, 1⅜, 1½, 1⅜) in [3 (3, 3.5, 3.5, 4, 3.5) cm] until 30 (30, 32, 32, 32, 34) sts rem.

Work around in k1, p1 ribbing for 2 in (5 cm) and BO in ribbing on last rnd.

### FINISHING

Weave in all ends neatly on WS.

Block by covering it with a damp towel; leave until completely dry.

Fluffy Bobble Pullover
for Adults ⟶

# Fluffy Bobble Pullover for Adults

An unbelievably light, soft, and warm pullover. It will also look great if oversized. For that plan, choose one or two sizes larger than usual.

*Level 2*

---

**Sizes:** XS (S, M, L, XL)

**FINISHED MEASUREMENTS**

Chest: Approx. 34½ (35½, 37½, 39½, 41¼) in [87.5 (90, 95, 100, 105) cm]

Total Length: Approx. 25½ (26½, 27¼, 27¼, 28) in [65 (67, 69, 69, 71) cm]

**MATERIALS**

**Yarn:** Sandnes Garn Børstet Alpakka (Brushed Alpaca) (CYCA #5 – bulky, 96% alpaca, 4% nylon, 120 yd (110 m) / 50 g)

Sandnes Garn KlompeLompe Merinoull [CYCA #3 – DK, light worsted, 100% Merino wool, 114 yd (104 m) / 50 g]

**YARN COLORS AND AMOUNTS:**

MC: Brushed Alpaca: Plum 4360: 350 (350, 350, 400, 400) g

CC: Merinoull, Powder Pink 4344: 50 (50, 50, 50, 50) g

**Needles:** U.S. size 8 (5 mm): 16 and 24 in (40 and 60 cm) circulars and set of 5 dpn; optional: 32 in (80 cm) circular for magic loop

**Gauge:** 16 sts in stockinette = 4 in (10 cm).

Adjust needle size to obtain correct gauge if necessary.

The bobbles are worked with Merinoull: *K1, p1, k1* in next st (= 3 sts into 1); turn, p3; turn, k3; turn, p2tog, p1; turn, k2tog.

The sweater is worked top down with Brushed Alpaca. The bobbles are worked with Merinoull.

With Brushed Alpaca and circular, CO 78 (80, 84, 88, 92) sts. Join, being careful not to twist cast-on row, pm for beginning of rnd. Work 8 rnds k1, p1 ribbing.

Knit 1 rnd, increasing 10 sts evenly spaced around = 88 (90, 94, 98, 102) sts.

Knit 2 (2, 3, 3, 4) rnds.

Knit 1 rnd, increasing 24 (22, 26, 30, 26) sts evenly spaced around = 112 (112, 120, 128, 128) sts.

Knit 1 rnd.

**Next Rnd (bobbles):** Knit with MC , working bobbles with CC as follows:

K1, bobble, *k3, bobble*; rep * to * around until 2 sts rem, k2.

Knit 3 rnds.

**Next Rnd (increase):** K1, M1, *k2, M1*; rep * to * around until 1 st rem, k1 = 168 (168, 180, 192, 192) sts.

Knit 1 (1, 2, 2, 3) rnds.

**Next Rnd (bobbles):** *K5, bobble*; rep * to * around.

Knit 5 (5, 6, 6, 7) rnds.

**Next Rnd (bobbles):** K8, bobble, *k11, bobble*; rep * to * around until 3 sts rem, k3.

Knit 1 rnd.

Knit 1 rnd, increasing 20 (26, 26, 26, 30) sts evenly spaced around = 188 (194, 206, 218, 222) sts.

Knit 4 (4, 6, 8, 10) rnds.

Knit 1 rnd, increasing 36 (34, 34, 34, 42) sts evenly spaced around = 224 (228, 240, 252, 264) sts.

Knit 2 (4, 6, 8, 10) rnds.

On next rnd, divide for body and sleeves:

K62 (64, 68, 72, 76), place next 50 (50, 52, 54, 56) sts on a holder for sleeve, CO 8 sts for underarm, k62 (64, 68, 72, 76), place next 50 (50, 52, 54, 56) sts on a holder for sleeve, CO 8 sts for underarm = 140 (144, 152, 160, 168) sts rem for body.

Work around in stockinette with Brushed Alpaca until body measures 23¾ (24½, 25¼, 25¼, 26) in [60 (62, 64, 64, 66) cm]. Finish with k1, p1 ribbing for 2 in (5 cm). BO in ribbing on last rnd.

### SLEEVES
Beginning at center of underarm, with dpn or magic loop circular, pick up and knit 4 sts, With dpn, pick up held 50 (50, 52, 54, 56) sts for sleeve, pick up and knit 4 sts on underarm. You are now at center of underarm – pm for beginning of rnd.

Knit around in stockinette until sleeve measures 19 in (48 cm) or desired length to cuff, **but**, when sleeve is 1¼ in (3 cm) long, begin shaping: K1, k2tog, knit until 3 sts rem, k2tog, k1.

Decrease the same way every 1⅜ in (3.5 cm) until 34 (34, 36, 40, 40) sts rem.

Work around in k1, p1 ribbing for 2 in (5 cm) and BO in ribbing on last rnd.

### FINISHING
Weave in all ends neatly on WS.

Block by covering it with a damp towel; leave until completely dry.

# Fluffy Bobble Doll's Jacket

Now mother, child, and baby doll can all wear the same sweater jacket. It's a quick-knit project on big needles, and it's guaranteed to be popular with the doll's mom.

*Level 2*

- - - - - - - - - - - - - - - - - - - - - - - - - - -

**Sizes:** One size doll (Baby Born)

**MATERIALS**
**Yarn:** Sandnes Garn Børstet Alpakka (Brushed Alpaca) (CYCA #5 – bulky, 96% alpaca, 4% nylon, 120 yd (110 m) / 50 g)

Sandnes Garn KlompeLompe Merinoull [CYCA #3 – DK, light worsted, 100% Merino wool, 114 yd (104 m) / 50 g]

**YARN COLORS AND AMOUNTS:**
MC: Brushed Alpaca: White 1001: 50 g

CC: Merinoull, Powder Rose 4032: 50 g

**Needles:** U.S. size 8 (5 mm): 16 in (40 cm) circular and set of 5 dpn; optional: 32 in (80 cm) circular for magic loop

**Notions:** 3 buttons

**Gauge:** 16 sts in stockinette = 4 in (10 cm).

Adjust needle size to obtain correct gauge if necessary.

- - - - - - - - - - - - - - - - - - - - - - - - - - -

The bobbles are worked with Merinoull: *K1, p1, k1* in next st (= 3 sts into 1); turn, p3; turn, k3; turn, p2tog, p1; turn, k2tog.

The sweater is worked bottom up, back and forth, with Brushed Alpaca.

With Brushed Alpaca and circular, CO 59 sts. Knit 8 rows = 4 garter ridges.

Continue back and forth in stockinette with 4 sts on each side in garter st for front bands.

Work 4 rows in stockinette and garter st bands.

**Next Row (bobbles):** K4, *k3, bobble*; rep * to * until 7 sts rem, k3, k4.

Work 5 rows in stockinette and garter st bands.

**Next Row (bobbles):** K4, k1, bobble, *k3, bobble*; rep * to * until 5 sts rem, k1, k4.

Work 5 rows in stockinette and garter st bands.

**Next Row (bobbles):** K4, k3, bobble, *k7, bobble*; rep * to * until 11 sts rem, k7, k4.

Continue in stockinette and garter bands until piece measures approx. 5¼ in (13 cm).

Shape underarms: K15, BO 4 sts, k21, BO 4 sts, k15.

**SLEEVES**
With Brushed Alpaca and dpn or magic loop, CO 20 sts. Divide sts onto dpn or on long circular and join; pm for beginning of rnd.

Knit 1 rnd, purl 1 rnd, knit 1 rnd, purl 1 rnd.

Continue sleeve in stockinette until it measures 3½ in (9 cm), **but**, when it is ¾ in (2 cm) long, begin shaping sleeve: K1, M1, knit until 1 st rem, M1, k1.

Increase the same way every 1¼ in (3 cm) until there are 26 sts total.

**Next Rnd:** BO 4 sts centered on underarm.

Set first sleeve aside while you make second sleeve the same way.

### YOKE
Begin on WS. Work across body, adding in sleeves at underarms. Work the outermost 4 sts at each side in garter st. Pm at each intersection of body and sleeve = 4 markers = 95 sts total.

**Note:** *At same time* as working yoke shaping, make buttonholes on right front band – the first one on 1st decrease row; 2nd one on 4th decrease row and, 3rd buttonhole on first ridge of neckband. Buttonhole: RS: K1, BO 2 sts. On following row, CO 2 sts over gap. <AUTHORS: Your pattern does not specify how to make the buttonholes or where – what is here is our guess. OK?>

On **each** RS row, decrease as follows: *Knit until 2 sts before marker, sl 1, k1, psso, sl m, k2tog.* Rep * to * at each marker; knit to end of row = 8 sts decreased.

Decrease the same way a total of 7 times = 39 sts rem.

After completing all decrease rows, finish with neckband: Knit 6 rows (= 3 garter ridges); don't forget last buttonhole. BO knitwise.

### FINISHING
Weave in all ends neatly on WS.

Seam underarms.

Sew on 3 buttons.

Block by covering it with a damp towel; leave until completely dry.

# Fluffy Bobble Sweater-Jacket

The ideal cozy sweater-jacket that both mother and daughter will love. It's light and comfy. The sweet bobbles can be made in a color matching the rest of the sweater, or maybe you prefer to choose your own striking color combination?

*Level 2*

- - - - - - - - - - - - - - - - - - - - - - - -

**Sizes:** 1 (2, 4, 6, 8, 10) years

**FINISHED MEASUREMENTS**
Chest: Approx. 22½ (24½, 25½, 28½, 30½, 32½) in [57.5 (62.5, 65, 72.5, 77.5, 82.5) cm]

Total Length: Approx. 13½ (14½, 17, 17¾, 20½, 22) in [34 (37, 43, 45, 52, 56) cm]

**MATERIALS**
**Yarn:** Sandnes Garn Børstet Alpakka (Brushed Alpaca) (CYCA #5 – bulky, 96% alpaca, 4% nylon, 120 yd (110 m) / 50 g)

Sandnes Garn KlompeLompe Merinoull [CYCA #3 – DK, light worsted, 100% Merino wool, 114 yd (104 m) / 50 g]

**YARN COLORS AND AMOUNTS:**
MC: Brushed Alpaca: Petroleum Blue 6075: 150 (150, 200, 250, 250, 250) g

CC: Merinoull, Light Petroleum Blue 6521: 50 (50, 50, 50, 50, 50) g or leftovers

**Needles:** U.S. size 8 (5 mm): 16 and 24 in (40 and 60 cm) circulars and set of 5 dpn; optional: 32 in (80 cm) circular for magic loop

**Notions:** 3 buttons

**Gauge:** 16 sts in stockinette = 4 in (10 cm).

Adjust needle size to obtain correct gauge if necessary.

- - - - - - - - - - - - - - - - - - - - - - - -

The bobbles are worked with Merinoull: *K1, p1, k1* in next st (= 3 sts into 1); turn, p3; turn, k3; turn, p2tog, p1; turn, k2tog.

The sweater is worked bottom up, back and forth, with Brushed Alpaca.

With Brushed Alpaca and circular, CO 105 (113, 121, 137, 145, 153) sts. Knit 8 rows = 4 garter ridges.

Continue back and forth in stockinette with 5 sts on each side in garter st for front bands.

Work 4 rows in stockinette and garter st bands.

**Next Row (bobbles):** K5, *k3, bobble*; rep * to * until 8 sts rem, k3, k5.

Work 5 rows in stockinette and garter st bands.

**Next Row (bobbles):** K5, k1, bobble, *k3, bobble*; rep * to * until 6 sts rem, k1, k5.

Work 5 rows in stockinette and garter st bands.

**Next Row (bobbles):** K5, k3, bobble, *k7, bobble*; rep * to * until 8 sts rem, k3, k5.

Work 7 rows in stockinette and garter st bands.

**Next Row (bobbles):** K5, *k7, bobble*; rep * to * until 12 sts rem, k7, k5.

Continue in stockinette and garter bands until piece measures approx. 7 in (18 cm).

**PLACE MARKERS:**

K27 (29, 31, 35, 37, 39), pm, k51 (55, 59, 67, 71, 75) for back, pm, k27 (29, 31, 35, 37, 39), pm.

**Next Row (RS):** Knit until 3 sts before marker, k2tog, k1, sl m, k1, k2tog. Rep decreases at each of the 4 markers = 101 (109, 117, 133, 141, 149) sts rem.

Continue in stockinette and garter bands until piece measures approx. 8 (8¼, 8¼, 8¾, 8¾, 9) in [20 (21, 21, 22, 22, 23) cm]. Decrease as above once more = 97 (105, 113, 129, 137, 145) sts rem.

**Note:** When piece measures 8¼ (9¾, 11, 12¼, 13½, 14¼) in [21 (25, 28, 31, 34, 36) cm], make the first buttonhole: K2, BO 2 sts, knit to end of row. On next row, CO 2 sts over the gap (you will make a total of 3 buttonholes on band).

Continue as est until piece measures 8¾ (10¼, 10¼, 10¼, 10¼, 11) in [22 (26, 26, 26, 26, 28) cm].

**Sizes 1 (2) years:** Shape underarms as described below and decrease as above on rem sizes = – (–, 109, 125, 133, 141) sts.

**Sizes 4 (6, 8, 10) years:** Continue as est until piece measures – (–, 11½ , 11½ , 12¼, 13) in [– (–, 29, 29, 31, 33) cm].

**Size 4 years only:** Shape underarms as described below and decrease as

above on rem sizes = – (–, –, 121, 129, 137) sts.

**Sizes 6 (8, 10) years:** Continue as est until piece measures – (–, –, 13 ,15, 16¼) in [– (–, –, 33, 38, 41) cm].

**ALL SIZES, SHAPE UNDERARMS:**
Shape underarms as follows: Knit until 4 sts before marker, BO 8 sts, knit until 4 sts before marker, BO 8 sts.

**SLEEVES**
With dpn or magic loop circular, CO 30 (30, 30, 32, 32, 34) sts.

Divide sts onto dpn or on long circular and join; pm for beginning of rnd.

Knit 1 rnd, purl 1 rnd, knit 1 rnd, purl 1 rnd.

Continue sleeve in stockinette until it measures 8¼ (9¾, 10¾, 12¼, 13½, 14½) in [21 (25, 27, 31, 34, 37) cm], **but**, when it is 2½ in (6 cm) long, begin shaping sleeve: K1, M1, knit until 1 st rem, M1, k1.

Increase the same way every 1¼ (1¼, 1⅜, 1⅜, 1⅜, 1½) in [3 (3, 3.5, 3.5, 3.5, 4) cm] until there are 38 (42, 42, 44, 46, 48) sts total.

**Next Rnd:** BO 8 sts centered on underarm.

Set first sleeve aside while you make second sleeve the same way.

**YOKE**
Begin on WS. Work across body, adding in sleeves at underarms. Work the outermost 5 sts at each side in garter st. Pm at each intersection of body and sleeve = 4 markers = 141 (157, 161, 177, 189, 201) sts total.

**Note:** *At same time* as working yoke shaping, make rem buttonholes on right front band – place 2nd buttonhole halfway through decrease rows and 3rd buttonhole on first ridge of neckband.

On each RS row, decrease as follows: *Knit until 2 sts before marker, sl 1, k1, psso, sl m, k2tog.* Rep * to * at each marker; knit to end of row = 8 sts decreased.

Decrease the same way a total of 11 (13, 13, 14, 15, 16) times = 53 (53, 57, 65, 69, 73) sts rem.

After completing all decrease rows, finish with neckband: Knit 6 rows (= 3 garter ridges); don't forget last buttonhole on first ridge. BO knitwise.

**FINISHING**
Weave in all ends neatly on WS.

Seam underarms.

Sew on 3 buttons.

Block by covering it with a damp towel; leave until completely dry.

# Fluffy Bobble Sweater-Jacket for Adults

*Level 2*

**Sizes:** XS (S, M, L, XL)

**FINISHED MEASUREMENTS**

Chest: Approx. 35½ (36¾, 38¼, 40¼, 42½) in [90 (93, 97.5, 102.5, 108) cm]

Total Length: Approx. 28¼ (28¾, 30¾, 31½, 32¼) in [72 (73, 78, 80, 82) cm]

**MATERIALS**

**Yarn:** Sandnes Garn Børstet Alpakka (Brushed Alpaca) (CYCA #5 – bulky, 96% alpaca, 4% nylon, 120 yd (110 m) / 50 g)

Sandnes Garn KlompeLompe Merinoull [CYCA #3 – DK, light worsted, 100% Merino wool, 114 yd (104 m) / 50 g]

**YARN COLORS AND AMOUNTS:**

MC: Brushed Alpaca: Petroleum Blue 6075: 350 (400, 450, 450, 450) g

CC: Merinoull, Light Petroleum Blue 6521: 50 (50, 50, 50, 50) g or leftovers

**Needles:** U.S. size 8 (5 mm): 16 and 24 or 32 in (40 and 60 or 80 cm) circulars and set of 5 dpn; optional: 32 in (80 cm) circular for magic loop

**Notions:** 3 buttons

**Gauge:** 16 sts in stockinette = 4 in (10 cm).

Adjust needle size to obtain correct gauge if necessary.

The bobbles are worked with Merinoull: *K1, p1, k1* in next st (= 3 sts into 1); turn, p3; turn, k3; turn, p2tog, p1; turn, k2tog.

The sweater is worked bottom up, back and forth, with Brushed Alpaca.

With Brushed Alpaca and circular, CO 169 (173, 181, 189, 197) sts. Knit 8 rows = 4 garter ridges.

Continue back and forth in stockinette with 5 sts on each side in garter st for front bands.

Work 4 rows in stockinette and garter st bands.

**Next Row (RS, bobbles):** K5, *k3, bobble*; rep * to * until 8 sts rem, k3, k5.

Work 5 rows in stockinette and garter st bands.

**Next Row (bobbles):** K5, k1, bobble, *k3, bobble*; rep * to * until 6 sts rem, k1, k5.

Work 5 rows in stockinette and garter st bands.

**Next Row (bobbles):** K5, k3, bobble, *k7, bobble*; rep * to * until 8 (12, 12, 12, 12) sts rem, k3 (7, 7, 7, 7), k5.

Work 7 rows in stockinette and garter st bands.

**Next Row (bobbles):** K5, *k7, bobble*; rep * to * until 12 (8, 8, 8, 8) sts rem, k7 (3, 3, 3, 3), k5.

Note: that the last bobble rows will not be symmetrical on all sizes.

Continue in stockinette and garter bands until piece measures approx. 9¾ in (25 cm).

### PLACE MARKERS:
K43 (44, 46, 48, 50), pm, k83 (85, 89, 93, 97) for back, pm, k43 (44, 46, 48, 50), pm.

**Next Row (RS):** Knit until 3 sts before marker, k2tog, k1, sl m, k1, k2tog. Rep decreases at each of the 4 markers. Decrease the same way every 2¾ in (7 cm) a total of 5 times = 149 (153, 161, 169, 177) sts rem.

**Note:** When piece measures 21¼ (21¼, 23¼, 23¼, 23¼) in [54 (54, 59, 59, 59) cm], and next row is on RS, make the first buttonhole: K2, BO 2 sts, knit to end of row. On next row, CO 2 sts over the gap (you will make a total of 3 buttonholes on band).

Continue as est until piece measures 21¾ (21¾, 23¾, 23¾, 23¾) in [55 (55, 60, 60, 60) cm].

Shape underarms as follows: Knit until 4 sts before marker, BO 8 sts, knit until 4 sts before marker, BO 8 sts.

### SLEEVES
With dpn or magic loop circular, CO 34 (34, 36, 40, 40) sts.

Divide sts onto dpn or on long circular and join; pm for beginning of rnd.

Knit 1 rnd, purl 1 rnd, knit 1 rnd, purl 1 rnd.

Continue sleeve in stockinette until it measures 19 in (48 cm) or desired length, **but**, when it is 2½ in (6 cm) long, begin shaping sleeve: K1, M1, knit until 1 st rem, M1, k1.

Increase the same way every 2 in (5 cm) until there are 50 (50, 52, 54, 56) sts total.

**Next Rnd:** BO 8 sts centered on underarm.

Set first sleeve aside while you make second sleeve the same way.

### YOKE
Begin on WS. Work across body, adding in sleeves at underarms. Work the outermost 5 sts at each side in garter st. Pm at each intersection of body and sleeve = 4 markers = 217 (221, 233, 245, 257) sts total.

**Note:** *At same time* as working yoke shaping, make rem buttonholes on right front band – place 2nd buttonhole halfway through decrease rows and 3rd buttonhole on first ridge of neckband.

On each RS row, decrease as follows: *Knit until 2 sts before marker, sl 1, k1, psso, sl m, k2tog.* Rep * to * at each marker; knit to end of row = 8 sts decreased.

Decrease the same way a total of 18 (18, 19, 20, 21) times = 73 (77, 81, 85, 89) sts rem.

After completing all decrease rows, finish with neckband: Knit 6 rows (= 3 garter ridges); don't forget last buttonhole on first ridge. BO knitwise.

## FINISHING

Weave in all ends neatly on WS.

Seam underarms.

Sew on 3 buttons.

Block by covering it with a damp towel; leave until completely dry.

# Dinosaur Doll Onesie

The doll also needs a stylish onesie for winter adventures and lounging in the stroller or baby carriage.

*Level 3*

**Sizes:** One size doll (Baby Born)

**MATERIALS**
**Yarn:** Sandnes Garn KlompeLompe Tynn Merinoull (fine Merino wool) [CYCA #1 – fingering, 100% Merino wool, 191 yd (175 m) / 50 g]

**YARN COLORS AND AMOUNTS:**
Color A: Blue-Petroleum 7251: 100 g

Color B: Putty 1013: 50 g or leftovers

**Needles:** U.S. sizes 1.5 and 2.5 (2.5 and 3 mm): 16 in (40 cm) circulars and sets of 5 dpn; optional: 32 in (80 cm) circular for magic loop

**Notions:** 5 buttons

**Gauge:** 27 sts on larger size needles = 4 in (10 cm).

Adjust needle size to obtain correct gauge if necessary.

The onesie is worked from the top down, beginning back and forth on a circular.

## BODY

With smaller size circular and color A, CO 53 sts. Work 6 rows back and forth in k1, p1 ribbing. Change to larger size circular. CO 6 sts for steek and begin working in the round. Knit 1 rnd, increasing 25 sts evenly spaced around (but do not increase in the 6 steek sts) = 78 sts. The steek sts are not included in stitch counts or shown on the chart.

Knit 1 rnd. Knit 1 rnd, increasing 35 sts evenly spaced around (but do not increase in the 6 steek sts) = 113 sts.

Now work following chart. After completing charted rows, you should have 127 sts.

Knit 1 rnd. Knit 1 rnd, increasing 14 sts evenly spaced around (but do not increase in the 6 steek sts) = 141 sts.

Knit 4 rnds.

On next rnd, divide for body and sleeves: K19, place 33 sts on a holder, CO 5 sts for underarm, k37, place 33 sts on a holder, CO 5 sts for underarm, k19 = 85 sts rem.

Continue around in stockinette until piece measures 7 in (18 cm). Knit 1 rnd and, *at the same time*, BO the 6 steek sts. On next rnd, place markers: K40, pm, k5, pm, k40, pm, CO 5 sts, pm = a marker on each side of the 5 front and 5 back sts.

Now increase 1 st (with M1) on each side of the 5 center front and 5 center back sts. Increase the same way on every other rnd a total of 3 times. Knit 1 rnd and, *at the same time*, BO the 5 center sts on front and back = 46 sts rem for each leg.

## LEGS

Work each leg separately. Knit around until leg is ⅝ in (1.5 cm) long. Begin leg shaping: K1, k2tog, knit until 3 sts rem, sl 1, k1, psso, k1. Decrease the same way every ⅝ in (1.5 cm) a total of 3 times = 40 sts rem. Continue in stockinette until leg

measures 4 in (10 cm). Knit 1 rnd, decreasing 10 sts evenly spaced around.

Make second leg the same way.

Change to smaller size dpn, Work 6 rnds k1, p1 ribbing and BO in ribbing on last rnd.

### SLEEVES
With larger size dpn and color A, beginning at center of the 5 sts you cast on for body, pick up and knit 3 sts, k33 held sts, pick up and knit 2 sts.

Knit around in stockinette until sleeve is 1 in (2.5 cm) long. Begin shaping sleeve:

K1, k2tog, knit until 3 sts rem, sl 1, k1, psso, k1. Decrease the same way every ¾ in (2 cm) until 32 sts rem and sleeve measures 3¼ in (8 cm).

Change to smaller size dpn and work 6 rnds k1, p1 ribbing; BO in ribbing on last rnd.

**Knitting Tip:** If you think it is difficult to pick up and knit sts, you can cast on sts instead and seam the opening with Kitchener st when finishing.

Knit second sleeve the same way.

### FINISHING TOUCHES
Reinforce steek by machine-sewing 2 fine lines on each side of center steek sts. Carefully cut open steek up center.

With color A (MC) and larger size needle, pick up and knit 3 sts for every 4 rows along right front edge. Work 6 rows k1, p1 ribbing; BO in ribbing on last row (make sure bind-off is not too tight).

Make left front band the same way, but, on 3rd row, make 5 buttonholes evenly spaced on band. Buttonhole: K2tog, yo.

Fold steek sts to WS and sew down with fine stitches. If it is difficult to get a smooth edging, you can knit a facing to cover cut edges. With color A and smaller size needle, pick up and knit sts along front edge as for front bands. Work back and forth in stockinette until facing is wide enough to cover steek. BO and sew down facing with same color as for onesie so the stitching will be invisible.

### FINISHING
Weave in all ends neatly on WS.

Stitch short ends of front bands down.

Sew on buttons.

Block by covering onesie with a damp towel; leave until completely dry.

■ Color A
□ Color B
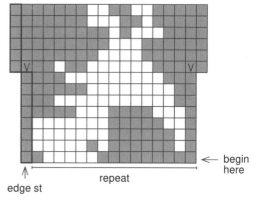
V increase here with M1

← begin here

↑ edge st    repeat

# Maiken Cap

A sturdy hat with nice detailing.

*Level 2*

**Sizes:** 3–6 (7–14 years, adult S/M, L/XL)

**MATERIALS**
**Yarn:** Sandnes Garn KlompeLompe Spøt [CYCA #3 – DK, light worsted, 40% Merino wool, 40% alpaca, 20% nylon, 147 yd (134 m) / 50 g]

**YARN COLORS AND AMOUNTS:**
Blue-Green 6871: 100 (100, 100, 100) g

**Needles:** U.S. sizes 6 and 8 (4 and 5 mm): 16 in (40 cm) circulars and sets of 5 dpn; optional: 32 in (80 cm) circular for magic loop

**Notions:** Optional – faux fur pom-pom

**Gauge:** 17 sts with yarn held double on larger size needles = 4 in (10 cm).

Adjust needle size to obtain correct gauge if necessary.

**STITCHES AND TECHNIQUES**
**RIGHT TWIST (RT)**
*Option 1:* Skip 1st st but leave it on left needle. Knit 2nd st in front of 1st st. Knit 1st st.

*Option 2:* Place 1st st on cable needle and hold in back of work. Knit 2nd st (in front of st on cable needle). K1 from cable needle.

**LEFT TWIST (LT)**
*Option 1:* Skip 1st st but leave it on left needle. Knit 2nd st in back of 1st st. Knit 1st st.

*Option 2:* Place 1st st on cable needle and hold in front of work. Knit 2nd st (behind st on cable needle). K1 from cable needle.

With 2 strands of yarn held together and smaller size circular, CO 74 (80, 80, 84) sts. Join, being careful not to twist cast-on row; pm for beginning of rnd. Work 8 (8, 12, 12) rnds k1, p1 ribbing.

Change to larger size circular.

Now purl the first 17 (20, 20, 22) sts and the last 17 (20, 20, 22) sts = back. Work in pattern on the center 40 sts. Pm on each side of the center 40 sts. On first rnd, increase 0 (0, 6, 6) sts evenly spaced across back = 34 (40, 46, 50) sts for back.

**PATTERN**
**Rnd 1:** *K1, p2*; rep * to * 4 times, k1, p14; rep * to * 4 times, k1.

**Rnd 2:** *Sl 1, p2*; rep * to * 4 times, sl 1, p14; rep * to * 4 times, sl 1.

Rep Rnds 1–2 a total of 4 times.

**Rnd 9:** *K1, p2*; rep * to * 3 times, LT, p1, LT, p12, RT, p1, RT, p2; rep * to * 2 times, k1.

**Rnd 10:** *Sl 1, p2*; rep * to * 3 times, p1, sl 1, p2, sl 1, p12, rep * to * 2 times, p1; rep * to * 2 times, sl 1.

**Rnd 11:** *K1, p2*; rep * to * 3 times, p1, LT, p1, LT, p10, RT, p1, RT, p3; rep * to * 2 times, k1.

**Rnd 12:** *Sl 1, p2*; rep * to * 3 times, p2, sl 1, p2, sl 1, p10, rep * to * 2 times, p2; rep * to * 2 times, sl 1.

**Rnd 13:** *K1, p2*; rep * to * 3 times, p2, LT, p1, LT, p8, RT, p1, RT, p4; rep * to * 2 times, k1.

**Rnd 14:** *Sl 1, p2*; rep * to * 3 times, p3, sl 1, p2, sl 1, p8, rep * to * 2 times, p3; rep * to * 2 times, sl 1.

**Rnd 15:** *K1, p2*; rep * to * 3 times, p3, LT, p1, LT, p6, RT, p1, RT, p5; rep * to * 2 times, k1.

**Rnd 16:** *Sl 1, p2*; rep * to * 3 times, p4, sl 1, p2, sl 1, p6, rep * to * 2 times, p4; rep * to * 2 times, sl 1.

**Rnd 17:** *K1, p2*; rep * to * 3 times, p4, LT, p1, LT, p4, RT, p1, RT, p6; rep * to * 2 times, k1.

**Rnd 18:** *Sl 1, p2*; rep * to * 3 times, p5, sl 1, p2, sl 1, p4, rep * to * 2 times, p5; rep * to * 2 times, sl 1.

**Rnd 19:** *K1, p2*; rep * to * 3 times, p5, LT, p1, LT, p2, RT, p1, RT, p7; rep * to * 2 times, k1.

**Rnd 20:** *Sl 1, p2*; rep * to * 3 times, p6, sl 1, p2, sl 1, p2, rep * to * 2 times, p6; rep * to * 2 times, sl 1.

**Rnd 21:** *K1, p2*; rep * to * 3 times, p6, LT, p1, LT, RT, p1, RT, p8; rep * to * 2 times, k1.

**Rnd 22:** *Sl 1, p2*; rep * to * 3 times, p7, sl 1, p2, sl 2, p2, sl 1, p9, rep * to * 2 times.

**Rnd 23:** *K1, p2*; rep * to * 3 times, p7, k1, p2, LT, p2, k1, p9; rep * to * 2 times, k1.

**Rnd 24:** *Sl 1, p2*; rep * to * 3 times, p7, sl 1, p2, sl 2, p2, sl 1, p9, rep * to * 2 times.

**Rnd 25:** *K1, p2*; rep * to * 3 times, p6, RT, p1, RT, LT, p1, LT, p8, rep * to * 2 times, k1.

**Rnd 26:** *Sl 1, p2*; rep * to * 3 times, p6, rep * to * 4 times, p6, rep * to * 2 times, sl 1.

**Rnd 27:** *K1, p2*; rep * to * 3 times, p6, rep * to * 4 times, p6, rep * to * 2 times, k1.

Rep Rnds 26–27 until cap measures 6⅛ (6¾, 7, 8) in [15.5 (17, 18, 20) cm].

Now knit every other rnd and, on alternate rnds, sl all knit sts and purl all purl sts. You should now have 3 purl sections on the back and 2 on the front.

**CROWN SHAPING**

Change to dpn when sts no longer fit around circular.

**Decrease Rnd 1:** Decrease 0 (6, 12, 16) sts evenly spaced across back purl section and 2 sts on each of the other 2 purl sections = 4 (10, 16, 20) sts decreased total.

Work 3 rnds.

**Decrease Rnd 2:** Decrease 6 sts evenly spaced across back purl section and 2 sts on each of the other 2 purl sections = 10 sts decreased total.

Work 3 rnds.

**Decrease Rnd 3:** Decrease 6 sts evenly spaced across back purl section and 2 sts on each of the other 2 purl sections = 10 sts decreased total.

Work 3 rnds.

**Decrease Rnd 4:** *P2, p2tog*; rep * to *, p3, k1, p2tog, k1, p2*; rep * to * 5 times, *p2tog, p2*; rep * to *, p1.

Purl 1 rnd.

**Decrease Rnd 5:** *P1, p2tog*; rep * to * 3 times, k1, p1, k1, p2tog*; rep * to * 5 times, *p1, p2tog*; rep * to *, p1.

Purl 1 rnd in pattern = last pattern rnd.

**Decrease Rnd 6:** *P2tog, p1*; rep * to * until 2 sts rem, p2.

Purl 1 rnd.

**Decrease Rnd 7:** *P2tog*; rep * to * around.

**FINISHING**

Cut yarn and draw end through rem sts; tighten.

Securely sew on pom-pom if desired.

Weave in all ends neatly on WS.

Block by covering cap with a damp towel; leave until completely dry.

139

# Julie Tunic

A charming winter tunic.
Perfect for wearing over jeans
and leggings.

*Level 2*

- - - - - - - - - - - - - - - - - - - - - - - - - -

**Sizes:** 6 months (1, 2, 4, 6, 8, 10 years)

**FINISHED MEASUREMENTS**
Chest: Approx. 22½ (23¾, 24¼, 26¾, 27¼, 29, 29¾) in [57 (60, 61.5, 68, 69, 73.5, 75.5) cm]

Total Length: Approx. 13½ (15¾, 16½, 18¼, 19¾, 22¾, 24½) in [34 (40, 42, 46, 50, 58, 62) cm]

**MATERIALS**
**Yarn:** Sandnes Garn KlompeLompe Spøt [CYCA #3 – DK, light worsted, 40% Merino wool, 40% alpaca, 20% nylon, 147 yd (134 m) / 50 g]

**YARN COLORS AND AMOUNTS:**
Flax Blue 6051: 150 (200, 200, 250, 300, 300, 350) g

**Needles:** U.S. sizes 2.5 and 4 (3 and 3.5 mm): 24 in (60 cm) circulars and sets of 5 dpn

**Gauge:** 22 sts on larger size needles = 4 in (10 cm).

Adjust needle size to obtain correct gauge if necessary.

- - - - - - - - - - - - - - - - - - - - - - - - - -

The tunic is worked from the top down.

With smaller size circular, CO 78 (80, 80, 82, 86, 86, 88) sts. Join, being careful not to twist cast-on row; pm for beginning of rnd. Work 6 (6, 8, 8, 8, 8, 8) rnds k1, p1 ribbing. Change to larger size circular.

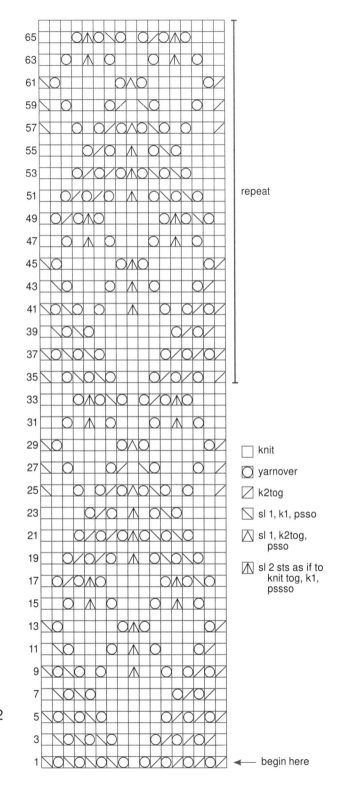

Legend:
- ☐ knit
- ⊙ yarnover
- ⧄ k2tog
- ⧅ sl 1, k1, psso
- ◹ sl 1, k2tog, psso
- ◸ sl 2 sts as if to knit tog, k1, pssso

← begin here

repeat

Knit 1 rnd, increasing (with M1) 26 (24, 24, 30, 26, 34, 32) sts evenly spaced around = 104 (104, 104, 112, 112, 120, 120) sts.

Pm for pattern (see chart): Pm, work 17 sts in pattern, pm, k35 (35, 35, 39, 39, 43, 43), pm, work 17 sts in pattern, pm, k35 (35, 35, 39, 39, 43, 43).

Continue as est, with 17 sts pattern between markers, and stockinette for rem sts.

Work 5 rnds.

On next rnd, increase 32 sts evenly spaced in stockinette sections (16 sts each on front and back).

Work 8 rnds.

On next rnd, increase 32 sts evenly spaced in stockinette sections (16 sts each on front and back).

**Sizes 4 (6, 8, 10) years:** Work 8 rnds.

On next rnd, increase 32 sts evenly spaced in stockinette sections (16 sts each on front and back).

**Sizes 8 (10) years:** Work 8 rnds.

On next rnd, increase 32 sts evenly spaced in stockinette sections (16 sts each on front and back).

**All sizes:** Work 10 rnds.

On next rnd, increase 22 (32, 44, 22, 32, 14, 26) sts evenly spaced in stockinette sections [11 (16, 22, 11, 16, 7, 13) sts each on front and back) = 190 (200, 212, 230, 240, 262, 274) sts.

Work 3 rnds.

Cut yarn and slip the last 11 (12, 14, 15, 17, 20, 22) sts to left needle. the rnd now begins here.

**Divide for sleeves:** Place the first 39 (41, 45, 47, 51, 57, 61) sts on a holder for sleeve, k56 (59, 61, 68, 69, 74, 76). Place next 39 (41, 45, 47, 51, 57, 61) sts on a holder for sleeve, k56 (59, 61, 68, 69, 74, 76).

Arrange sts of front and back on one circular, and, at the same time, CO 7 sts for each underarm = a total of 126 (132, 136, 150, 152, 162, 166) sts. Mark st at center of each underarm as a marked st.

## FRONT AND BACK

Knit in the round in stockinette until piece measures 11¾ (14¼, 15, 16¼, 17¾, 20½, 22) in [30 (36, 38, 41, 45, 52, 56) cm], **but**, after 1¼ in (3 cm), increase as follows: *Knit to marker, M1, k1, M1*; rep * to * once more = 4 sts increased.

Increase the same way every 1½ in (4 cm) a total of 4 (5, 5, 6, 6, 7, 8) times.

Change to smaller size circular and work in k1, p1 ribbing for 1½ (1½, 1½, 2, 2, 2½, 2½) in [4 (4, 4, 5, 5, 6, 6) cm]. BO in ribbing on last rnd.

## SLEEVES

With larger size dpn, pick up and knit 4 sts on underarm, work 39 (41, 45, 47, 51, 57, 61) sts from holder, pick up and knit 3 sts on underarm. Pm on first st as a marked st and always purl that st. Work sleeve in the round.

After working as est for 1 in (2.5 cm), P1 (marked st), k2tog, work as est until 2 sts rem, sl 1, k1, psso. Decrease the same way every 1 (1, 1¼, 1⅜, 1⅜, 1, 1) in [2.5 (2.5, 3, 3.5, 3.5, 2.5, 2.5) cm] until 32 (34, 38, 40, 42, 42, 44) sts rem.

Continue as est without decreasing until sleeve measures 7 (8, 9½, 11½, 12¼, 13¾, 15) in [18 (20, 24, 29, 31, 35, 38) cm] or desired length. Change to smaller size dpn and work around in k1, p1 ribbing for 1½ (1½, 1½, 2, 2, 2½, 2½) in [4 (4, 4, 5, 5, 6, 6) cm]. BO in ribbing on last rnd.

Make second sleeve the same way.

## FINISHING

Weave in all ends neatly on WS.

Block by covering tunic with a damp towel; leave until completely dry.

# Thick "Shoe" Socks

This Norwegian style of heavy socks is called "tykke lubber" (or "kjokke lobber" as we say on our island of Karmøy).

## Level 1

**Sizes:** 0–1 (3–6, 9–12 months, 1–2 years)

**MATERIALS**
**Yarn:** Sandnes Garn KlompeLompe Merinoull [CYCA #3 – DK, light worsted, 100% Merino wool, 114 yd (104 m) / 50 g]

**YARN COLORS AND AMOUNTS:**
Soft Purple 4331: 50 (50, 50, 50) g

**Needles:** U.S. size 4 (3.5 mm): set of 5 dpn

**Notions:** 4 buttons

**Gauge:** 22 sts = 4 in (10 cm).

Adjust needle size to obtain correct gauge if necessary.

The socks are worked back and forth on two dpn.

CO 27 (31, 35, 37) sts. Knit 1 row.

**Increase Row 1:** K1, M1, k12 (14, 16, 17), M1, k1, M1, k12 (14, 16, 17), M1, k1.

Knit 1 row.

**Increase Row 2:** K1, M1, k13 (15, 17, 18), M1, k3, M1, k13 (15, 17, 18), M1, k1.

Knit 1 row.

**Increase Row 3:** K1, M1, k14 (16, 18, 19), M1, k5, M1, k14 (16, 18, 19), M1, k1.

Knit 1 row.

**Increase Row 4:** K1, M1, k15 (17, 19, 20), M1, k1, M1, k5, M1, k1, M1, k15 (17, 19, 20), M1, k1.

Knit 5 rows.

**Decrease Row 1:** K17 (19, 21, 22), K2tog, k7, k2tog, k17 (19, 21, 22).

Knit 1 row.

**Decrease Row 2:** K16 (18, 20, 21), K2tog, k7, k2tog, k16 (18, 20, 21).

Knit 1 row.

**Decrease Row 3:** K15 (17, 19, 20), K2tog, k7, k2tog, k15 (17, 19, 20).

Knit 1 row.

**Decrease Row 4:** K14 (16, 18, 19), K2tog, k2tog, k3, k2tog, k2tog, k14 (16, 18, 19).

Knit 1 row.

**Decrease Row 5:** K15 (17, 19, 20), K2tog, k1, k2tog, k15 (17, 19, 20).

Knit 1 row.

**Decrease Row 6:** K12 (14, 16, 17), K2tog, k2tog, k1, k2tog, k2tog, k12 (14, 16, 17).

Knit 1 row.

**Decrease Row 7:** K10 (12, 14, 15), K2tog, k2tog, sl 1, k2tog, psso, k2tog, k10 (12, 14, 15) = 24 (28, 32, 34) sts rem.

Now join to work in the round.

Work 30 (30, 34, 34) rnds in k1, p1 ribbing and BO loosely in ribbing on last rnd.

**FINISHING**

Seam sock on sole and back of heel.

Weave in all ends neatly on WS.

Fold ribbed cuff in half and sew on 2 buttons at the side, stitching through both layers of cuff.

Make second sock the same way.

Block by covering socks with a damp towel; leave until completely dry.

# Big Sister's Cap

A dress-up cap with a fun bow in versions for doll, baby, and child.

*Level 2*

**Sizes:** One size doll (6 months, 1–2, 3–6, 7–10 years)

**MATERIALS**

**Yarn:** Sandnes Garn KlompeLompe Merinoull [CYCA #3 – DK, light worsted, 100% Merino wool, 114 yd (104 m) / 50 g]

**YARN COLORS AND AMOUNTS:**
Soft Purple 4331: 50 (100, 100, 100, 100) g

**Needles:** U.S. size 4 (3.5 mm): 16 in (40 cm) circular and set of 5 dpn

**Gauge:** 22 sts = 4 in (10 cm).

Adjust needle size to obtain correct gauge if necessary.

**STITCHES AND TECHNIQUES**

**Elongated knit stitch (ek):** Knit 1 between the k2tog and 1 slipped st 2 rounds below, k1, pulling loop up with right needle tip to elongate it. Work the next ek in same hole. See video at klompelompe.no.

With circular, CO 12 (24, 24, 24, 24) sts. Work in garter st (knit all rows) on the outermost 2 (4, 4, 4, 4) sts at each side and work in pattern on the center 8 (16, 16, 16, 16) sts.

**PATTERN**

**Row 1:** *K2tog, sl 1, k1 psso, k4*; rep * to * across pattern section.

**Row 2:** Purl across pattern section.

**Row 3:** *1 ek, k2, 1 ek, k4*; rep * to * across pattern section.

**Row 4:** Purl across pattern section.

**Row 5:** *K4, k2tog, sl 1, k1, psso*; rep * to * across pattern section.

**Row 6:** Purl across pattern section.

**Row 7:** *K4, 1 ek, k2, 1 ek*; rep * to * across pattern section.

**Row 8:** Purl across pattern section.

Work as est until piece measures approx. 15 (17¾, 18¼, 18½, 19) in [38 (45, 46, 47, 48) cm] and next row is either Row 4 or 8 of pattern (on WS). Continue as follows:

**Doll size:** K2, p3, BO 2 sts, p3, k2. On next row knit across and CO 2 new sts over gap.

**Next Row:** K2, p8, k2. Continue in pattern as before for about 2½ in (6 cm). BO in pattern on either Row 4 or 8.

**All Baby and Child sizes:** K4, p6, BO 4 sts, p6, k4. On next row knit across and CO 4 new sts over gap.

**Next Row:** K4, p16, k4. Continue in pattern as before for about 3½ in (9 cm). BO in pattern on either Row 4 or 8.

**All sizes:** Draw the end through the hole and sew securely to opening. Weave in ends neatly on WS. Twist the yarn many times round the middle (at the opening). Fold in the corners on the bow ends and sew them together. Finally, tack down the bow ends well with a few stitches.

148

Pick up and knit sts along top edge, beginning at center back. Pick up 1 st in each st but skip every 3rd up to the knot of the bow, CO 2 sts, pick up and knit same number of sts as on first side to center back. Knit 1 rnd, adjusting stitch count to 72 (88, 92, 96, 100) sts.

Work in stockinette until piece measures 3½ (5¼, 6, 6¾, 7½) in [9 (13, 15, 17, 19) cm].

Knit 1 rnd, decreasing 0 (0, 4, 0, 4) sts evenly spaced around.

**SHAPE CROWN**
(change to dpn when sts no longer it around circular)**:**

**Decrease Rnd 1:** *K6, k2tog*; rep * to * around.
Knit 2 rnds.

**Decrease Rnd 2:** *K5, k2tog*; rep * to * around.
Knit 2 rnds.

**Decrease Rnd 3:** *K4, k2tog*; rep * to * around.
Knit 2 rnds.

**Decrease Rnd 4:** *K3, k2tog*; rep * to * around.

**Decrease Rnd 5:** *K6, k2tog*; rep * to * around, ending with k4 (4, 4, 0, 0).

**Decrease Rnd 6:** *K5, k2tog*; rep * to * around, ending with k4 (4, 4, 0, 0).

**Decrease Rnd 7:** *K4, k2tog*; rep * to * around, ending with k4 (4, 4, 0, 0).

**Decrease Rnd 8:** *K3, k2tog*; rep * to * around, ending with k4 (4, 4, 0, 0).

**Decrease Rnd 9:** *K2, k2tog*; rep * to * around.

**Decrease Rnd 10:** *K2tog*; rep * to * around, ending with k1 (0, 0, 0, 0).

Cut yarn and draw end through rem sts; tighten.

**FINISHING**
Weave in all ends neatly on WS.

Block by covering cap with a damp towel; leave until completely dry.

Dinosaur ⟶
Union Suit

# Dinosaur Union Suit

Nursery school's coolest guy will be running around
with dinosaurs on his outfit!

*Level 3*

**Sizes:** 1–3 (6–9 months, 1, 2 years)

**FINISHED MEASUREMENTS**

Chest: Approx. 18¼ (19, 21½, 22¾) in [46 (48, 54.5, 58) cm]

Total Length: Approx. 19¼ (22, 25½, 28¼) in [49 (56, 65, 72) cm]

**MATERIALS**

**Yarn:** Sandnes Garn KlompeLompe Spøt [CYCA #3 – DK, light worsted, 40% Merino wool, 40% alpaca, 20% nylon, 147 yd (134 m) / 50 g]

**YARN COLORS AND AMOUNTS:**

Color A (MC): Blue-Petroleum 7251: 150 (200, 250, 250) g

Color B (CC): Putty 1013: 50 (50, 50, 50) g or leftovers

**Needles:** U.S. sizes 2.5 and 4 (3 and 3.5 mm): 16 and 24 in (40 and 60 cm) circulars and sets of 5 dpn

**Notions:** 6 (7, 7, 8) buttons

**Gauge:** 22 sts on larger size needles = 4 in (10 cm).

Adjust needle size to obtain correct gauge if necessary.

The union suit is worked from the top down, beginning back and forth on a circular.

**BODY**

With smaller size circular and color A, CO 69 (73, 73, 77) sts. Work back and forth in k1, p1 ribbing for 1¼ in (3 cm). Change to larger size circular. CO 6 sts for steek and begin working in the round. The steek sts are not included in stitch counts or shown on the chart. Do not work increases or decreases in steek sts. Knit 1 rnd, increasing 30 (32, 38, 42) sts evenly spaced around (but do not increase in the 6 steek sts) = 99 (105, 111, 119) sts.

Knit 4 (4, 7, 7) rnds. Knit 1 rnd, increasing 24 (26, 34, 30) sts evenly spaced around = 123 (131, 145, 149) sts.

Knit 4 (4, 7, 7) rnds. Knit 1 rnd, increasing 28 (35, 36, 32) sts evenly spaced around = 151 (168, 181, 181) sts.

Now work following chart. After completing charted rows, there should be 171 (188, 205, 205) sts. Knit 0 (1, 2, 4) rnds with color A. Knit 1 more rnd, adjusting stitch count to 176 (184, 202, 214) sts.

Knit 1 rnd. Knit 1 rnd, increasing 14 sts evenly spaced around = 141 sts.

On next rnd, divide for body and sleeves: K20 (21, 25, 27), place next 44 (46, 48, 50) sts on a holder, CO 7 sts for underarm, k48 (50, 56, 60), place next 44 (46, 48, 50) sts on a holder, CO 7 sts for underarm, k20 (21, 25, 27) + steek sts.

## FRONT AND BACK

There should be 102 (106, 120, 128) sts for body.

Continue around in stockinette and color A until piece measures 11½ (13, 14½, 16¼) in [29 (33, 37, 41) cm]. Knit 1 rnd and, *at the same time*, BO the 6 steek sts.

On next rnd, place markers: K48 (50, 57, 61), pm, k6, pm, k48 (50, 57, 61), pm, CO 6 sts, pm = a marker on each side of the 6 front and 6 back sts.

Now increase 1 st (with M1) on each side of the center 6 front and 6 back sts. Increase the same way on every other rnd a total of 4 (4, 5, 6) times. Knit 1 rnd and, *at the same time*, BO the 6 center sts on front and back = 56 (58, 67, 73) sts rem for each leg.

## LEGS

Work each leg separately. Pm at crotch. Knit around until leg is ¾ in (2 cm) long. Begin leg shaping: Knit until 3 sts before marker, sl 1, k1, psso, knit until 1 st after marker, k2tog. Decrease the same way every 1 (1¼, 1¼, 1¼) in [2.5 (3, 3, 3) cm] a total of 5 (5, 6, 8) times = 46 (48, 55, 57) sts rem. Continue in stockinette until leg measures 5¼ (6¾, 8, 9½) in [13 (17, 20, 24) cm]. Knit 1 rnd, decreasing 12 (10 , 13, 15) sts evenly spaced around = 34 (38, 42, 42) sts rem.

Change to smaller size dpn, Work 16 rnds k1, p1 ribbing and BO in ribbing on last rnd.

Make second leg the same way.

## SLEEVES

With larger size dpn and color A, beginning at center of the 7 sts you cast on for body, pick up and knit 4 sts, k44 (46, 48, 50) held sts, pick up and knit 3 sts. Divide sts onto dpn. The first st is a marked st and always purled.

Knit around in stockinette (don't forget to purl marked st) until sleeve is 1 (1¼, 1⅜, 1⅜) in [2.5 (3, 3.5, 3.5) cm] long. Begin shaping sleeve:

Knit until 2 sts before marked st, sl 1, k1, psso, purl marked st, k2tog. Decrease the same way every 1 in (2.5 cm) until 41 (41, 43, 43) sts rem. Continue without further shaping until sleeve measures 5¼ (6¼, 7½, 8¾) in [13 (16, 19, 22) cm].

Knit 1 rnd, decreasing to eliminate marked st. Knit next rnd, decreasing 6 (4, 6, 4) sts evenly spaced around = 34 (36, 36, 38) sts rem.

Change to smaller size dpn and work 16 rnds k1, p1 ribbing; BO in ribbing on last rnd.

Knit second sleeve the same way.

## FINISHING TOUCHES

Reinforce steek by machine-sewing 2 fine lines on each side of center steek sts. Carefully cut open steek up center.

**Front bands:** On boy's version, make buttonholes on left front band, and, for girls, on right band.

With color A (MC) and smaller size needle, pick up and knit 3 sts for every 4 rows along front edge. Button band: Work 8 rows k1, p1 ribbing; BO in ribbing on last row (make sure bind-off is not too tight).

Make buttonhole band the same way, but, on 3rd row, make 6 (7, 7, 8) buttonholes evenly spaced on band. Buttonhole: BO 2 sts. On next row, CO 2 sts over each gap.

Fold steek sts to WS and sew down with fine stitches. If it is difficult to get a smooth edging, you can knit a facing to cover cut edges. With color A and smaller size needle, pick up and knit sts along front edge as for front bands. Work back and forth in stockinette until facing is wide enough to cover steek. BO and sew down facing with same color as for onesie so the stitching will be invisible.

## FINISHING

Weave in all ends neatly on WS. Stitch short ends of front bands down. Sew on buttons. Block by covering onesie with a damp towel; leave until completely dry.

---

**Knitting Tip:** If you think it is difficult to pick up and knit sts, you can cast on sts instead and seam the opening with Kitchener st when finishing.

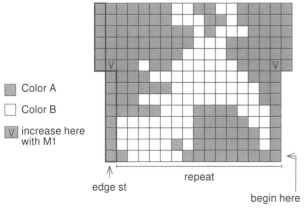

Color A

Color B

V increase here
with M1

↑
edge st

repeat

begin here →

# Dinosaur Earflap Cap

A cap with tough dinosaurs, perfectly matching the pullover or union suit with the same pattern. The cap fits the head well and keeps ears warm with good earflaps.

*Level 2*

---

**Sizes:** 0–2 (3–5, 6–12 months, 1–3, 3–6 years)

**MATERIALS**
**Yarn:** Sandnes Garn KlompeLompe Spøt [CYCA #3 – DK, light worsted, 40% Merino wool, 40% alpaca, 20% nylon, 147 yd (134 m) / 50 g]

**YARN COLORS AND AMOUNTS:**
Color A: Blue-Green 6871: 50 (50, 50, 50, 50) g

Color B: Putty 1013: 50 (50, 50, 50) g or leftovers

**Needles:** U.S. sizes 2.5 and 4 (3 and 3.5 mm): 16 in (40 cm) circulars and set of 5 dpn in larger size

**Gauge:** 22 sts on larger size needles = 4 in (10 cm).

Adjust needle size to obtain correct gauge if necessary

---

The cap begins with the I-cord ties on the earflaps.

With color A and smaller size dpn, CO 4 sts. Make an I-cord 7 in (18 cm) long.

**I-CORD**
With a dpn, knit the sts. *Do not turn. Slide the sts back to front of needle, bring yarn across WS, and knit the sts. *Rep from * to * until cord is desired length (see video at klompelompe.no).

Now begin increasing for the first earflap:

**Row 1, WS:** *P1, k1, M1, k1, p1.

**Row 2, RS:** (P1 in front loop and k1 in back loop) of next st, p1, k1, p1 (k1 in front loop and p1 in back loop) of next st.

**Row 3:** Work in k1, p1 ribbing across.

**Row 4, RS:** (K1 in front loop and p1 in back loop) of next st, k1, p1, k1, p1, k1, (p1 in front loop and k1 in back loop) of next st.

**Row 5:** Work in p1, k1 ribbing across.

Continue, increasing as est until there are 17 (19,19, 21, 21) sts. Work last row on WS. Set first earflap aside and make a second one the same way.

With smaller size circular, CO 6 sts, work across first earflap, CO 23 (23, 31, 31) sts, work second earflap, CO 5 sts = 68 (72, 80, 84, 88) sts total.

Join and work 10 rnds k1, p1 ribbing. Change to larger size circular. Knit 1 rnd, increasing 12 (8, 10, 6, 8) sts evenly spaced around = 80 (80, 90, 90, 96) sts.

Knit 2 rnds.

Now work following chart. After completing charted rows, continue in stockinette with color A until cap measures 4 (4¾, 5¼ 5¾, 6½) in [10 (12, 13, 14.5, 16.5) cm]. Knit 1 rnd, decreasing 8 (8, 10, 2, 8) sts evenly spaced around = 72 (72, 80, 88, 88) sts rem.

On next rnd, begin shaping crown (change to dpn when sts no longer fit around circular):

**Decrease Rnd 1:** *K6, k2tog*; rep * to * around.
Knit 2 rnds.

**Decrease Rnd 2:** *K5, k2tog*; rep * to * around.
Knit 2 rnds.

**Decrease Rnd 3:** *K4, k2tog*; rep * to * around.
Knit 2 rnds.

**Decrease Rnd 4:** *K3, k2tog*; rep * to * around.

**Decrease Rnd 5:** *K6, k2tog*; rep * to * around, ending with k4 (4, 0, 4, 4).

**Decrease Rnd 6:** *K5, k2tog*; rep * to * around, ending with k4 (4, 0, 4, 4).

**Decrease Rnd 7:** *K4, k2tog*; rep * to * around, ending with k4 (4, 0, 4, 4).

**Decrease Rnd 8:** *K3, k2tog*; rep * to * around, ending with k4 (4, 0, 4, 4).

**Decrease Rnd 9:** *K2, k2tog*; rep * to * around.

**Decrease Rnd 10:** *K2tog*; rep * to * around, ending with k1 (1, 0, 0, 0).

Cut yarn and draw end through rem sts; tighten.

**FINISHING**
Weave in all ends neatly on WS.

Block cap by covering it with a damp towel; leave until completely dry.

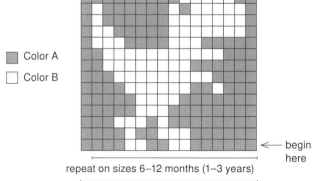

■ Color A
□ Color B

← begin here

repeat on sizes 6–12 months (1–3 years)

repeat on sizes 0–2 months (3–5 months, 3–6 years)

# Cable and Rib Cap

A cap that fits perfectly. The ribbing hugs the face well and gradually extends all the way around.

*Level 2*

**Sizes:** 3–5 (6–12 months, 1–2, 3–6 years)

**MATERIALS**

**Yarn:** Sandnes Garn KlompeLompe Merinoull [CYCA #3 – DK, light worsted, 100% Merino wool, 114 yd (104 m) / 50 g]

**YARN COLORS AND AMOUNTS:**
Powder Pink 4344: 50 (50, 100, 100) g

**Needles:** U.S. size 2.5 and 4 (3 and 3.5 mm): 16 in (40 cm) circular in larger size and sets of 5 dpn

**Notions:** Optional – faux fur pom-pom

**Gauge:** 22 sts on larger size needles = 4 in (10 cm).

Adjust needle size to obtain correct gauge if necessary.

With larger size circular, CO 70 (80, 90, 90) sts. Join, being careful not to twist cast-on row; pm for beginning of rnd.

Begin working around in pattern:

**Rnds 1–2:** *K5, p1, k1, p1, k1, p1*; rep * to * around.

**Rnd 3:** *K5, p1, yo,k1, p1, k1, slip yo over, p1*; rep * to * around.

Rep Rnds 1–3 10 (12, 13,14) times.

**CROWN SHAPING**
Change to dpn when sts no longer fit around circular.

**Decrease Rnd 1:** *K3, k2tog*; rep * to * in each knit panel and continue pattern as est in rem "cable" panels.

Work 2 rnds in pattern, with k4 in stockinette panels.

**Decrease Rnd 2:** Sl 1, k1, psso, k2*; rep * to * in each stockinette panel and continue pattern as est in rem "cable" panel.

Work 2 rnds in pattern, with k3 in stockinette panels.

**Decrease Rnd 3:** *K1, k2tog*; rep * to * in each knit panel and continue pattern as est in rem "cable" panels.

Work 2 rnds in pattern, with k2 in stockinette panels.

**Decrease Rnd 4:** *K2tog*; rep * to * in each knit panel and continue pattern as est in rem "cable" panels.

Work 1 rnd in pattern, with k1 in stockinette panels.

**Decrease Rnd 5:** *K1, k2tog*; rep * to * around.

Knit 1 rnd.

**Decrease Rnd 6:** *K2tog*; rep * to * around.

**Sizes 6–12 months (1–2, 3–6 years):** K2tog around.

Cut yarn and draw end through rem sts; tighten.

**EARFLAPS**
Make 2 earflaps with 11 sts between them at back. Th 3rd st of rnd is center back.

With larger size dpn, pick up and knit 16 (18, 20, 20) sts for one earflap.

Work 3 rows in stockinette.

**Next Row, RS:** K1, k2tog, knit until 3 sts rem, sl 1, k1, psso, k1.

Purl 1 row.

Decrease as above on every RS row until 4 sts rem. Purl alternate rows.

**Last Row:** K2tog, k2tog tbl.

Slip rem 2 sts to a holder. Make second earflap the same way.

### RIBBING
With larger size circular, pick up and knit 13 (15, 17, 17) sts on right earflap, 27 (33, 39, 39) sts between earflaps on front of cap, and 13 (15, 17, 17) sts on left earflap. Change to smaller size needle. Work 4 rows k1, p1 ribbing and BO in ribbing on last row.

Pick up and knit 3 sts on end of ribbing and knit the 2 sts from holder.

Purl 1 row.

**Next Row:** K1, sl 1, k2tog, psso, k1.

Knit rem 3 sts into an I-cord 7 in (18 cm) long.

Finish other earflap the same way.

### RIBBING ON BACK NECK
With smaller size needle, pick up and knit 11 sts between earflaps on back. Work 4 rows k1, p1 ribbing back and forth. BO on in ribbing on last row.

### FINISHING
Sew sides of ribbing to earflaps.

Weave in all ends neatly on WS.

Block cap by covering it with a damp towel; leave until completely dry.

Optional: Securely sew on faux fur pom-pom to top of cap.

# Little Troll Doll Pants

Amusing pants with a texture pattern, for a doll.

*Level 2*

**Sizes:** One size doll (Baby Born)

**MATERIALS**
**Yarn:** Sandnes Garn KlompeLompe Merinoull [CYCA #3 – DK, light worsted, 100% Merino wool, 114 yd (104 m) / 50 g]

**YARN COLORS AND AMOUNTS:**
Powder Pink 4344: 100 g

**Needles:** U.S. sizes 2.5 and 4 (3 and 3.5 mm): 16 in (40 cm) circulars and sets of 5 dpn

**Crochet Hook:** U.S. size C-2 (2.5 mm)

**Notions:** 2 buttons

**Gauge:** 22 sts on larger size needles = 4 in (10 cm).

Adjust needle size to obtain correct gauge if necessary.

The pants are worked top down.

With smaller size circular, CO 74 sts. Join, being careful not to twist cast-on row; pm for beginning of rnd. Work around in k1, p1 ribbing for 9 rnds, **but**, on the 4th rnd, make 2 buttonholes at the front. Work 30 sts in ribbing, BO 2 sts, work 10 sts in ribbing, BO 2 sts, work 30 sts in ribbing. On next rnd, CO 2 sts over each gap.

Change to larger size needle, Knit 1 rnd, increasing 10 sts evenly spaced around = 84 sts.

Now raise back with short rows.

**Note:** There is a yarnover after each turn; when you later come to one, knit/purl the yarnover with next st).

K10; turn, yo. P20; turn, yo. K25; turn, yo. P30; turn, yo. Knit to beginning of rnd.

Begin working in texture pattern:

**Rnd 1:** *Sl 3 st purlwise wyf, p3*; rep * to * around.

**Rnd 2:** Work as for Rnd 1.

**Rnds 3–5:** Knit.

**Rnd 6:** K1, *K1 tog with the 2 strands from Rnds 1 and 2, k5*; rep * to * around until 5 sts rem, k1 tog with the 2 strands from Rnds 1 and 2, k4.

**Rnd 7:** *P3, sl 3 st purlwise wyf*; rep * to * around.

**Rnd 8:** Work as for Rnd 7.

**Rnds 9–11:** Knit.

**Rnd 12:** K4, *K1 tog with the 2 strands from Rnds 7 and 8, k5*; rep * to * around until 2 sts rem, k1 tog with the 2 strands from Rnds 7 and 8, k1.

**Rep Rnds 1–12.**

Continue in pattern until body measures 5¼ in (13 cm) down

front of pants and the next rnd is 6 or 12 in pattern.

On the next rnd, decrease as follows: BO 3 sts, work 36 sts in pattern, BO 6 sts, work 36 sts in pattern, BO 3 sts.

Work each leg separately = 36 sts for each leg. Pm for beginning of rnd. Work 6 rnds in pattern.

Change to stockinette. After working for ⅜ in (1 cm), begin shaping leg as follows: K1, k2tog, knit until 3 sts rem sl 1, k1, psso, k1.

Decrease the same way every ⅜ in (1 cm) a total of 3 times. Continue in stockinette until leg measures 2½ in (6 cm). Work 12 rnds in pattern. Knit 1 rnd, decreasing 4 sts evenly spaced around = 26 sts rem.

Change to smaller size dpn. Work 10 rnds in k1, p1 ribbing. BO in ribbing on last rnd.

Make second leg the same way.

Make an I-cord (see video at klompelompe. no). With larger size dpn, CO 4 sts. Knit the sts. *Do not turn. Slide the sts back to front of needle, bring yarn across WS, and knit the sts.*Rep from * to * until cord is approx. 14¼ in (36 cm) long. Make second I-cord the same way.

Sew the center of the cord securely at center back of pants. Crochet a button loop at each end of the cord: ch 6, attach chain with sl st (measure to make sure chain is long enough for button. Sew a button to the cord approx. 2 in (5 cm) from the end. Bring the cord through the buttonhole from back to front.

**FINISHING**
Weave in all ends neatly on WS.

Block pants by covering with a damp towel; leave until completely dry.

# Izzy Cap with Two Pom-Poms

A cozy cap with two sweet pom-poms and a two-color pattern.
It's a perfect match for the Izzy polar bear pullover, but also
a fun accessory to a single-color garment.

*Level 2*

**Sizes:** 6–12 months (1–2, 3–4 years)

**MATERIALS**
**Yarn:** Sandnes Garn KlompeLompe Spøt [CYCA #3 – DK, light worsted, 40% Merino wool, 40% alpaca, 20% nylon, 147 yd (134 m) / 50 g]

**YARN COLORS AND AMOUNTS:**
Color A: Putty 1013: 50 (50, 50) g

Color B: Light Soft Purple 4321: 50 (50, 50) g

**Needles:** U.S. sizes 2.5 and 6 (3 and 4 mm): 16 in (40 cm) circulars + extra larger size needle for bind-off

**Notions:** 2 faux fur pompoms

**Gauge:** 22 sts on larger size needles = 4 in (10 cm).

Adjust needle size to obtain correct gauge if necessary

With color A and smaller size circular, CO 80 (84 84) sts. Join, being careful not to twist cast-on row; pm for beginning of rnd. Work 10 rnds in k1, p1 ribbing.

Change to larger size circular and color B. Knit 1 rnd, increasing 10 (11, 16) sts evenly spaced around = 90 (95, 100) sts.

Now work following charted pattern until cap measures 6¼ (7, 8) in [16 (18, 20) cm] and ends with a complete motif.

Turn cap inside out. Fold so that at beginning and end of row face each other. Join with three-needle bind-off.

With larger size needle, k2tog, joining first st on each needle. *K2tog with 1 st from each needle. Pass first worked st on right needle over second.* Rep from * to * until all sts have been bound off.

Cut yarn.

**FINISHING**
Turn cap right side out and securely attach a pom-pom to each tip.

Weave in all ends neatly on WS.

Block cap by covering (except pom-poms) with a damp towel; leave until completely dry.

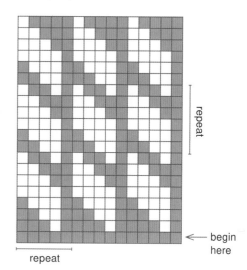

☐ Color A
■ Color B

repeat

repeat

← begin here

# Index

| | | | | |
|---|---|---|---|---|
| Albertine Cap | 86 | Izzy Cap | 102 |
| Big Sister's Cap | 148 | Izzy Cap with | |
| Blanket for the | | Two Pom-Poms | 164 |
| Smallest Ones | 54 | Izzy Polar Bear Pullover | 104 |
| Cable and Rib Cap | 158 | Julie Tunic | 141 |
| Dinosaur Doll Onesie | 132 | Julie Turtleneck Pullover | 90 |
| Dinosaur Earflap Cap | 156 | Kari Coat | 108 |
| Dinosaur Onesie | 39 | Kurt Pants | 61 |
| Dinosaur Pullover | 56 | Lighthouse Pullover | 51 |
| Dinosaur Union Suit | 152 | Little Troll Doll Pants | 162 |
| Dottie Deer Pullover | 94 | Little Troll Pants | 98 |
| Easy Mittens | 20 | Maiken Cap | 136 |
| Fluffy Bobble Doll's Jacket | 124 | Nerigjønå Cap | 26 |
| Fluffy Bobble Pullover | 118 | Nerigjønå Cowl | 22 |
| Fluffy Bobble Pullover | | Nordigjønå Cap | 18 |
| for Adults | 122 | Nordigjønå Cowl | 17 |
| Fluffy Bobble Sweater-Jacket | 126 | Olle Ball Cap | 76 |
| Fluffy Bobble Sweater-Jacket | | Rambaskår Pants | 70 |
| for Adults | 129 | Rambaskår | |
| Flutter-About Scarf | 74 | Sweater-Jacket | 64 |
| Grandmother's Dream Cap | 9 | Super-Easy Poncho | 46 |
| Grandmother's Dream | | Thick "Shoe" Socks | 145 |
| Sweater-Jacket | 11 | Wing Dress | 29 |
| Henry Felted Mittens | 92 | Wing Dress for Dolls | 34 |
| Hubbabubba Cap | 44 | Wing Union Suit | 80 |
| Hubbabubba Cowl | 42 | Winter Sweet Skirt | 114 |

# Acknowledgments

We have a superb group of test knitters, and, once more, we thank all of them for their invaluable contributions.

Test knitters: Marianne Hartwedt, Gunn Marit Hølland, Britt Alise Kvalevaag Stange, Johanna F. K. Gismervik, Mary Therese Utvik, Kristine Høvring, Randi Andreassen, Svanhild Andreassen, Ingebjørg Thorsen, Tina Kvilhaug, Astrid Apeland Thorsen, Linda Andreassen, Aina Pedersen, Hege B. Hamre, Nancy Hetland, Rakel Bergjord, Sissel Eikeland, Berthe Rossabø, Liv Gismervik, Gunn Nordis R. Ekornrud, Ingrid Gudmundsen, Ida Helland, Vibeke E. Lindtner, Line F. Taranger, Stina Steingildra, Aina Kristin Størkersen, Ida O. Kvalevaag, Rhonda H. Nes, Åse Osmundsen, Synnøve Nymark, Ingrid H. Hiller, Silje K. Berge, Tove Kalstø Milje, Gunnvor Thulin, Mette Brinchmann, Ingrid J. D. Bergland, Gro Torunn Utvik, Liv Syre, Ragnhild Omvik, Karen Qvale, Renate Helgen, Katherine Hettervik, Eva B. Kvalevaag, Elinor Nyvoll, Edith Qvale, and Caroline Lillesund.

Many thanks to all our charming models: David, Tor Eliah, Adrian, Margrete, Magnus, Noah, Samuel, Jostein, Helene B., Helene A. E., Elida, Olivia, Thale, Tora, Tilda, Sebastian, Leon, Henrik, Andrea, Theodor, Ariel, Ida, Anna Elise, Marie, Rebecca, Amelia, Wina, and Nora Martine.

Thank you many times over to Sandnes Garn, who provided test yarn and produced such fantastic yarns for us.

We also wish to thank our fantastic publisher, and, in particular, our always positive editor, Solveig Øye. After six books, we still have the same good feelings, and it is always so easy to work together with them.

We also want to give a big thank-you to Anne Vines, who once more produced such a fine design for our book.